THE FILM PHOTONOVEL

WORLD COMICS AND GRAPHIC NONFICTION SERIES
Frederick Luis Aldama and Christopher González, editors

The World Comics and Graphic Nonfiction series includes monographs and edited volumes that focus on the analysis and interpretation of comic books and graphic nonfiction from around the world. The books published in the series use analytical approaches from literature, art history, cultural studies, communication studies, media studies, and film studies, among other fields, to help define the comic book studies field at a time of great vitality and growth.

THE FILM PHOTONOVEL

A Cultural History of Forgotten Adaptations

Jan Baetens

UNIVERSITY OF TEXAS PRESS AUSTIN

Printed in the United States of America
First edition, 2019

Requests for permission to reproduce material from this work should be sent to:
Permissions
University of Texas Press
P.O. Box 7819
Austin, TX 78713-7819
utpress.utexas.edu/rp-form

♾ The paper used in this book meets the minimum requirements of ANSI/NISO Z39.48-1992 (R1997) (Permanence of Paper).

LIBRARY OF CONGRESS CATALOGING-IN-PUBLICATION DATA

Names: Baetens, Jan, author.
Title: The film photonovel : a cultural history of forgotten adaptations / Jan Baetens.
Other titles: World comics and graphic nonfiction series.
Description: First edition. | Austin : University of Texas Press, 2019. | Series: World comics and graphic nonfiction series | Includes bibliographical references and index.
Identifiers: LCCN 2018031172 | ISBN 978-1-4773-1822-5 (cloth : alk. paper) | ISBN 978-1-4773-1823-2 (library e-book) | ISBN 978-1-4773-1824-9 (nonlibrary e-book)
Subjects: LCSH: Fotonovelas—History and criticism. | Film adaptations—History and criticism. | Motion pictures and literature.
Classification: LCC PN6714 .B35 2019 | DDC 741.5/9—dc23
LC record available at https://lccn.loc.gov/2018031172

doi:10.7560/318225

Contents

Illustrations

Acknowledgments

Many individuals and institutions have to be thanked for their invaluable help and support.

First of all, I thank Frederick Aldama, editor of the World Comics and Graphic Nonfiction Series, who encouraged my project from its first stuttering until its final form. Equal thanks are due to the two anonymous reviewers of the manuscript as well as to Jessica Rutherford and Kip Keller for having carefully read and edited the text. It was a privilege to work with all of you.

As I was writing this book, many colleagues and specialists in the field generously offered time and space for discussion, and I have greatly benefited from their insights and erudition: Alain Boillat (Lausanne), Geert Buelens (Utrecht), Philippe Capart (Brussels), David Filipe (Wexner Center for the Arts, Ohio State University), Michel Delville (Liège), Giovanni Fiorentino (Viterbo), Guido Furci (Paris), Luke Gartlan (St. Andrews, Scotland), Tara Kreider (Thompson Library, Ohio State University), William Horrigan (Wexner Center for the Arts, Ohio State University), Donata Meneghelli (Bologna), Susan Liberator (Billy Ireland Cartoon Library, Ohio State University), David Pinho Barros (Porto), Marie-Françoise Plissart (Brussels), Domingo Sánchez-Mesa (Granada), and Bruno Takodjerad

(Paris). Special thanks to Stefania Giovenco (Paris), who introduced me to the hidden continent of the film photonovel; Clarissa Colangelo (Leuven), who was the first reader of the first complete draft; and Hugo Frey (Chichester), my partner in crime in so many graphic-narrative adventures.

My work on this book has been largely facilitated by a generous grant from the Flemish Science Foundation (FWO Vlaanderen) for a sabbatical leave during the academic year 2016–2017.

THE FILM PHOTONOVEL

1 / Excavating the Film Photonovel

To most readers, the subject of this book may appear to be a cultural UFO, and with good reason. The film photonovel—the term that I will use to refer to this hybrid genre—and the magazines that specialized in this noncanonical genre ceased to exist many decades ago, and in most cases, they have been not only overlooked but also forgotten. The cultural area where the film photonovel was read was limited: mainly Italy and France, and to a smaller extent neighboring countries, such as Spain and Belgium, as well as certain parts of Latin America. Moreover, the material is not easy to access, for only a very few specialized archives collect it, and the opportunities to find good, diverse, and affordable material remnants of the once-flourishing film-photonovel trade via traditional or online marketplaces—auctions, flea markets, garage sales, retail venues specializing in pulp fiction, and eBay—remain rare. For this reason, without personal contacts, alternative archives maintained by fans, a lot of chance, and, once in a while, a little help from my friends, I could never have written this book.

Generally speaking, the film photonovel is a genre at the crossroads of two other genres: first, the *film novel*, the retelling in prose of a movie's narrative (sometimes illustrated)—a genre as old as cinema and still alive in various forms all over the world; second, the *photonovel*—typically a European photographic romance genre published in women's magazines after World War II. The form enjoyed its greatest success between 1947 (when the first photonovels appeared on the market) and the mid-1960s, when the rapidly increasing penetration of television screens in households dramatically affected the impact and circulation of this much-contested and heavily debated genre. Photonovels still exist, but they no longer have the presence and social influence that they had in their first twenty years. One might consider, therefore, the film photonovel—sometimes confusingly called *fumetti* in the United States[1]—to be the photographic equivalent of the *novelization*, a specialized subgenre of the broader field of the traditional film novel. More precisely, the film photonovel is a film-novel subgenre remediated under the influence of the photonovel. Historically, the genre was short-lived, reaching its height in the period between 1950 and 1964. I address this heyday later on.

This book logically builds on earlier studies of the photonovel (Baetens 2010, 2013) and novelization (Baetens 2005, 2008). It is, however, anything but a continuation or expansion of that research, because while working on the photonovel and novelization, I was largely unaware that the film photonovel existed; it was still a hidden continent for me. Back then I did not even identify as unique in their own right the few film photonovels that I knew. In this sense, this book is, for me, a fresh start, and I am grateful to all those—from the anonymous "authors" of the film photonovels to the many friends, colleagues, open-minded antiquarians, and collectors—who helped me build and expand my collection (yes, life sometimes resembles *Treasure Island*)—and fostered my interest in this new field. The world of the film photonovel regularly proves the value of "rogue archivists" (De Kosnik 2016), who build their collections from the bottom up, fueled by the energy of a gift economy, often heedless of the academic rules of the game—archive building, copyright management, and scholarly detachment, for example—but driven by a passion and a commitment that reshape official history.

An example of a radically lowbrow, throwaway pulp subgenre, the film photonovel has not been stored in traditional archives. Many of these works are located in public archives that keep the magazines that published this kind of material, but archivists did not use the tag "film photonovel" in their catalogue cards (this is also the case for novelizations, which are likewise not easy to trace). Commercial archives of the publishers that produced and distributed the film photonovels are incomplete, and most of the companies no longer exist. Smaller publishers did not maintain archives, because of the extreme volatility of the business, in which bankruptcy and takeovers were the rule rather than the exception. Thus, there are tremendous gaps in many files and collections. It should be noted that "general" publishers, that is, those that did not specialize in women's magazines, were often reluctant to mention their production of photonovels in their backlists and promotional material (Bravo 2003, 125),[2] and most of them did not capitalize on the popularity of the film photonovel, which peaked around 1955. Their interest in the photonovel was purely financial, and given the smaller sales figures of the film photonovel, most of them did not want to invest in this highly competitive and risky field. Moreover, they were afraid that the poor reputation of both the photonovel and the film photonovel would negatively influence the image of their traditional literary output.

At first sight, the film photonovel is an object that, although despised and overlooked, offers plenty to those in film and literature studies who are interested in forms and cultures of hybridization. It raises interesting questions for genre studies and gender studies, too. And the material—as I hope will become clear in the rest of this book—is appealing, even seducing and intriguing. Unlike most other formerly ostracized genres that were eventually included in mainstream scholarship (the best example here is comics, but other noncanonical genres such as science fiction, the detective novel, children's literature, romance, horror, and pornography come to mind, all of which now have specialized academic journals), the film photonovel has never been central to literary and cultural studies. Hence the question, why has this hybrid genre been historically marginalized from the traditional canons that have come to dominate these fields? It is a paradox, given the commercial profitability of the film photonovel: in the ten years of its existence as a successful format in the popular press,[3] the film photonovel was big business.

In the period 1955–1965, first in Italy, then in France, and occasionally in Spain and Portugal, a significant number of magazines published film photonovels weekly, semimonthly, or monthly. Around 1955, some twenty magazines were competing for readers at newsstands (Morreale 2007b), but as early as 1957, the market was deep in crisis. At the end of the decade, at least thirty magazines were competing in France (Ghera 2006). These figures are startling, as is the number of readers, which was a multiple of the copies sold at newsstands, since film photonovels and other popular magazines were widely shared. In Italy, the all-time best seller seems to have been the 1954 film-photonovel version of *Ulisse/Ulysses*, a 1954 Lux/Paramount peplum film (a sword-and-sandals movie) produced by Dino De Laurentiis, directed by Mario Camerini, and starring Kirk Douglas and Silvana Mangano: 500,000 copies were sold in Italy (Amelio 2007, 14).[4]

In France, the monthly print run of one of the market leaders, *Nous Deux Film*, part of the photonovel empire published by Les Éditions mondiales, was 140,000 copies—a profitable number that had shrunk to 58,000 by 1963, when the publication ended (Antonutti 2013, 145). In comparison with the print runs of the photonovels of that period (Giet 1997; Bravo 2003), these figures are rather modest, but it is necessary to note the number of magazines in this niche and the significant social circulation of the copies. Michele Mercuri, whose father was the CEO of a photonovel company that also "did" film photonovels, mentions the quite reliable figure of "millions of readers" weekly during the mid-1950s in Italy (Mercuri 2007).

At the same time, serious limits on distribution may explain the rapid disappearance of the film photonovel from collective memory. First, these magazines were sold mainly at newsstands, which relegated them to the status of other disposable press items. Further, film photonovels were more expensive than photonovels, a comparable type of publication. In 1955, the flagship film-photonovel series *Cineromanzo Gigante* or *I Vostri Film Romanzo* cost 150 lire, while the three leading photonovel magazines, *Grand Hôtel*, *Bolero-Film*, and *Sogno*, cost 30, 40, and 30 lire, respectively.[5] This difference in price certainly explains the comparatively low print runs of all film-photonovel magazines. On the other hand, as will be discussed in detail later on, film photonovels were used in a variety of ways—for instance, as pinup and poster resources, images that were cut out and transformed into pictures to be put on the wall, an informal appropriation that was also a key factor in the material disappearance of these magazines.

To overcome the limitations of newsstand sales, most magazines promoted subscription policies, although other barriers appeared. Not least, this type of purchase was too expensive for the targeted audience, which could afford to buy film photonovels weekly at best, depending on the household's budget, which was very limited in the 1950s (by the time that popular audiences started benefiting from the economic boom of the 1960s, the film photonovel as a genre had disappeared). In addition, film photonovels, unlike photonovels, were almost never published in installments, but rather as "complete films," which reduced the need to subscribe. Another problem was that the editorial policy of most magazines was unselective regarding genres and styles: almost anything could end up as a film photonovel. Publishing such a diversity of magazines was not an effective strategy for attracting subscribers, as can be deduced from the heterogeneity of the material sold via used-magazines channels; it is almost impossible to find all issues of a given magazine for a given year.

A second reason for the limited flourishing of the film photonovel was its circumscribed geographic reach. Although the film photonovel was a virtually universal format, it existed mainly in two countries, with some smaller ripple effects in parts of the world, such as Argentina, that were open to Franco-Italian influences, often thanks to migrant communities. There were examples of film photonovels in non-European countries, both before and after the golden age of the film photonovel, but they were unsystematic and always rather short-lived. For example, in the United States in 1964, James Warren's *Famous Films #2* was a forty-two-page volume titled "Curse of Frankenstein / Horror of Dracula," which drew on a film-photonovel technique (and the same magazine probably released other similar issues). In the United States in the 1970s (before the VCR), film photonovels, mainly of sci-fi movies, flourished in pocket-book format (Muir 2005). These works were, however, called photonovels, not film photonovels, most likely because the photonovel genre itself did not have any known US equivalent, at least not as it had been popularized in Europe. A similar confusion between photonovels and film photonovels was pervasive in Latin American productions. In a discussion of the *fotonovela* (photonovel), one reads, for instance:

> Initially produced in Italy and Spain, *fotonovelas* were tactile representations of the movie with which they correlated. The documented history of the *fotonovela* is varied, although the Hispanic/Latino *fotonovela* dates back to the early 1940's in correlation with the rise in the popularity of film. Eventually, Latin American countries began developing *fotonovelas* that featured original stories that were not based on cinema productions. By the 1960's, approximately 23 movies were featured in the *fotonovela* format and nearly three times as many *fotonovelas* with original content were circulating throughout Mexico, Central and South America. Toward the late 1980's, Mexico was publishing approximately 70 million *fotonovelas* per month. (Edwards 2016; bibliographic citations in the original have been omitted)

In South Africa, where nonlocally produced television programs were introduced only in the 1970s, popular magazines in the 1960s published film-photonovel serials based on foreign television material.[6] Television as a primary resource for these kinds of adaptations was briefly popular in the early 1980s, for example, with the famous *Dallas* serial.[7] In none of these cases, however, was there a direct link with the Italian or the French culture of production of film photonovels, and this gap undoubtedly accelerated the rapid forgetting of the genre. In the absence of an appropriate genre label, it is difficult to acknowledge the continuity and change between all these practices; and because most of the publications came and went without leaving many traces, it becomes nearly impossible to compile a comprehensive archive or even to vaguely suggest what may bring together the diverse experiments and practices in this field.

The most important reason for the rapid and lasting disappearance of the film photonovel, however, was its strong association with the photonovel, another noncanonical literary genre that continues to suffer from status problems as well as an almost complete absence from English-speaking countries, which makes it a "bad" object for so-called global literary studies. The photonovel, often discarded as a romance comic with pictures—I will come back to this misreading—has remained an understudied genre subject to sociological and political prejudices. The photonovel is the prototypical example of "bad" reading: one of the worst specimens of the culture industry, an ignominious vehicle for spreading reactionary propaganda and a tool for manipulating its victimized female and semiliterate audiences. For reasons I will discuss further, the film photonovel, which encompassed most of the visual forms and mechanisms of the photonovel, was considered even more embarrassing than its model. According to Emiliano Morreale, currently the director of the Cinemateca Nazionale in Rome, it was seen as the "lumpen" version of the photonovel (Morreale 2007a, 207), a crude judgment by which he hinted at the unacceptable degradation of the filmic original, often an art house movie, by the codes of the photonovel. Romance lovers may have accepted, even encouraged, the transformation of a movie into a melodrama. Cinephiles, on the contrary, raged against the adaptation of their much-loved films in film-photonovel canvases. Morreale's bleak vision is much more than a personal stance, which he takes great care to nuance and fine-tune. The rejection of the film photonovel is a widely shared a priori in film criticism and theory. As noted by Serge Ghera, there is only one known example of a film journal, *Midi-Minuit Fantastique* (1962–1972), that acknowledged the existence of these kinds of publications and that used them for a review, in spite of the fact that, in a large majority of the cases, film photonovels were the only possible way to have and to keep a substantial visual trace of a certain movie.[8] It should be noted that when the journal was launched, the classic film photonovel was about to disappear from newsstands, surviving only in the niche genres covered by *Midi-Minuit Fantastique*—science fiction, horror, fantasy—which reduces the impact of the acknowledgment.

The general dislike of the film photonovel explains both the quasi absence of serious research in the field and the difficulty of finding reliable archives. This is a problem for many noncanonical genres and practices, but the case of the film photonovel is extreme. At the same time, this book is proof of the vitality and resilience of the communities that share a passion for the film photonovel. Even in scholarship, the return of the film photonovel is something that goes beyond the personal taste of certain individuals. The study of under-researched genres such as that of the film photonovel is a necessary complement to official histories that document the relationships between cinema and literature, all too hastily reduced to the subfield of book-to-film adaptations (Quaresima 2004).

What, then, is at stake in this book? First, it ties in with the recent broadening and widening of adaptation studies. Thanks to the landmark publications of scholars such as Simone Murray (2012), who has reframed the practice of adaptation as part of the larger cultural industry of global (art house) film production, and Jean-Louis Jeannelle (2016), whose concept of "adaptability" makes a plea for a much broader approach than the one-to-one comparison between book and film in actual adaptations, there is now room for the study of adaptation as a cultural practice—a paradigm shift increasingly visible in translation and literary studies and encouraged by the move toward new, more contextualized approaches in film history. Thus, the first aim of this book is to make a modest contribution to a new reading of the cultural history of the relationships between film and literature.

A second ambition concerns a debate in genre and medium studies, which are, in more than one aspect, a single field. No reading of genre should ignore issues of medium structures, and vice versa: medium—in the twofold sense of material host medium and "cultural form" or "cultural practice," as defined by Raymond Williams ([1970] 1974)—and genre are mutually dependent and inextricably linked concepts. There is no medium without proper content, and genre is an essential parameter of this concept. It is c not a coincidence that chief theoreticians such as Stanley Cavell—ironically?—struggle with the terminology and tend to go back and forth between medium and genre (see Cavell 1979). Conversely, no genre can be thought of without taking into account the medium structure that allows it to socially exist. Genre changes often correspond to medium changes; hence, the rise of the "material-historical medium theory" in literary studies, as Thérenty (2007) calls it, and the implementation of this dimension in genre theory (Baetens et al. 2015). From this point of view, this book participates in the ongoing debate about the material history of the interaction between film and literature. Hence its particular emphasis on a lesser-known genre within this larger history, the film photonovel; on the relationships between this genre and the medium aspects of its form; and on its publication context. To read the film photonovel is one thing; to read it as part of a particular magazine is another.

Finally, the specific methodological framework of this book is that of comparative textual media (Hayles and Pressman 2013). This approach is media focused, which requires that all cultural productions, including traditional print documents, be considered media. It is comparative, which means that cultural documents and practices are analyzed via a comparison with other practices and documents, both synchronically and diachronically, and with the help of more than one disciplinary framework. And its emphasis on the textual should not be interpreted narrowly as referring only to print or only to verbal language, but as referring to the fact that the notion of "text" may encompass a wide range of media forms and practices.

A last word on the corpus used in this study: as already intimated, the production of the film photonovel was impressive, with an average of at least twenty-five to thirty magazines in business in the period 1955–1965. They poured out works at least monthly—the gaps in the archives are too prominent to allow for firm speculation, but one can easily imagine the exceptional size of the corpus. For this reason, it is necessary to take a closer look at global tendencies within the film-photonovel market as well as to work with a representative and available sample. In the appendix is an overview, as comprehensive as possible, of the magazines active in the photo-film business during the years studied here, as well as a detailed description of the works that I read during the research for this book, which span the gamut in the field. The analysis highlights the types of publishers and series active in the market. The analysis and the case studies on which it is based cross boundaries between European and US films, art house movies and blockbuster cinema, B movies and expensive productions, and purely local and globally released and marketed films. To make connections outside Europe, I end the book with some brief notes on American film photonovels.

2 / A Brief History of the Film Photonovel

Is it possible to write the history of the film photonovel? The answer to this deceivingly simple question is both yes and no. Yes, because the film photonovel exists and the publishing history of its magazines sharply defines a beginning, middle, and end for the genre. The presence of some ambiguous or hard-to-qualify examples does not jeopardize the robustness of this history (all genres present such cases). But also no—and in a sense, this is more interesting than the yes—because one cannot write the history of the film photonovel without also writing the history of the larger field in which it emerged, triumphed, declined, and vanished. And this, of course, is an open and unending story, which the history of the film photonovel only further complicates.

Any brief sketch of this expanded field immediately raises questions regarding the internal and external intricacies of the notion of film. No movie can be detached, either synchronically or and diachronically, from others of the same genres. Throughout cinema history there have been many types of films. From the very beginning, the dichotomy between the Lumière brothers and Georges Méliès, as well as between documentary and fiction, for example, represents a significant cinematographic ecology that never stopped producing or establishing new distinctions. In recent scholarship, these linear and teleological simplifications have increasingly come under attack (Elsaesser 2009); within the brief history of the film photonovel outlined here, the history of cinema is clearly a never-ending story of "deaths" and "rebirths" (Gaudreault and Marion [2013] 2015).

Moreover, film intersects with many other practices—in this case, literature. This relationship is complex, with a multiplicity of incarnations. Initially, we can understand the encounter between page and screen as one of conflict and competition. Remediation theory (Bolter and Grusin 1999) insists on the supersession of "older" media—for instance, popular lowbrow fiction or mainstream narrative—by "new" forms of storytelling, such as cinema, which adapts literary sources into visual formats that appear to be more widely consumed than their verbal sources. But the struggle between old and new media is ongoing, evinced by the conflict between film and television. We see this, for example, in today's "complex television" (Mittell 2015), which has remediated some of the narrative capacities of cinema. Meanwhile, literature has been developing new models and fashions that enable it to strike back and reposition itself, even in the field of popular fiction, where it seems to have lost its appeal (Collins 2010).

In practice, this means that the history of the film photonovel has to be written in reference to a whole range of film and literature genres, but also to a wide array of publication media or formats—a still only partially charted continent that Leonardo Quaresima and others have called "narrated cinema" (Quaresima 2004; De Berti 2000). Some examples of relevant genres are readers' digests, novelizations, director's interviews, film reviews, fan magazines, film novels in general, "making of" books or reports, scripts, celebrity biographies, and gossip sections. These are genres that were quite familiar to the reader of the film photonovel, if only because all of them were widely published in film-photonovel magazines, where they constituted part of the genre's "paratext."[1] Some examples of media, in addition to a whole series of publications in print, are producers' catalogues that describe and illustrate movies; other promotional material, including, for instance, still photographs used for publicity in theater lobbies and film posters; unpublished material such as storyboards; and the treatment of the film photonovel in movies, documentaries, and fictional works. Finally, it is important to keep an eye on the cultural dominants of the period one is investigating. If the years around 1960 prove to have a special relevance for the film photonovel, one should not forget that these were also years both of crisis for the traditional studio system and of the success of more independent filmmaking, for instance, that of the New Wave or Left Bank cinema. Additionally, they were the years when auteur theory was rapidly institutionalized and when there was a rapid spread of certain genres that exemplified and reinforced the newly established cultural authority of the director as author, that is, as a cultural agent who used the camera as a pen to communicate and impose a worldview. Among these new genres were the published script—that is, a rewritten and published version of the script that was derived from the final cut—and the interview book, preferably devoted to an auteur's whole oeuvre (de Baecque [2002] 2013). In this regard, the anonymous character of practically all known film photonovels, including those based on movies made by self-conscious and ambitious young filmmakers, is something that immediately comes to the fore. A historical and institutional study of the genre, therefore, cannot evade the question of who is actually the author of a film photonovel.

Step 1: The Drawn Novel

After World War II, the European magazine business underwent a complete and rapid reconstruction. These changes were most notable in women's weeklies. In the prewar tendencies and favorites (fashion and housekeeping, celebrity gossip and romance) that persisted, one notices the direct influence of American marketing techniques and genre models, such as the strong attraction of "true confession" magazines, which first appeared in the United States in the 1930s. The most striking feature, however, was a sharper awareness of the tension between the overt politicization of many postwar publications and the apparently nonpolitical stance of a new type of women's magazine that unashamedly displayed a craving for "only entertainment."[2]

In the postwar period—marked by extreme poverty, unemployment, continued rationing (of paper, for example), and tremendous political tensions—not all new magazine entrepreneurs could depend on public funding or subsidies to produce their publications. Most governments proved very suspicious of magazines allegedly celebrating the American way of life, as was the case with romance magazines. For these entrepreneurs, it was crucial to tap as forcefully as possible into the public's preferences. But to bet on readers' desire to escape the war's lasting miseries and the postwar period's growing disappointments was not an adequate strategy for attracting readers to newsstands. New editorial and marketing strategies would be necessary. The first was purely economic: new price points, designed to appeal to readers who formerly could not afford to buy magazines. The second strategy was a cultural one: the development of new content for the well-established market of women's magazines. This twofold strategy was the unique selling proposal of Cino Del Duca, the creator of the magazine *Grand Hôtel*, which dominated the newsstands from its launch on 29 June 1946, setting the standard for the most successful woman's magazine format for the next two decades (Antonutti 2013; Cardone 2004a), first in Italy and soon thereafter in France, where *Nous Deux* (Both of us),[3] initially the sister magazine of *Grand Hôtel*, appeared on 14 May 1947 (Faber, Minuit, and Takodjerad 2012). The Del Duca empire offered a magazine that cost a third of what competing magazines charged at the time (namely, 12 lire, which is approximately US$0.31). A simple market study had brought him to the conclusion that the new magazine had to be a merger of the two genres, which had never previously been done: that is, a hybrid of comics and romance, or more specifically in the European context, a melodrama.

The new weekly *Grand Hôtel* (named for the famous 1932 film with Greta Garbo, based on a best-selling novel of 1928 by Vicky Baum) was a tiny, poorly printed sixteen-page magazine, but above all, it was a completely new genre, the "drawn novel" (Baetens 2017b). The genre resembled a comic, but it was also indebted to the world of cinema and illustrated film novels. The story in a drawn novel pretends to have been inspired by a Hollywood movie. Its drawings (color wash drawings, technically speaking) aspire to be photorealistic copies of film stills, and the faces of its protagonists simply copy those of famous movie stars, which were ubiquitous on European screens after the war. (The Nazis had banned the showing of US films.)

At first sight, one might think that the drawn novel is just a local form of a romance comic, but this is not the case. First, the American line of romance comics was not launched until 1948, and its visual style was very cartoonish, whereas that of the drawn novel was, from the beginning, thoroughly cinematographic, both stylistically and in content. In addition, drawn novels have a rather suspect intertextual status: they are neither originals nor adaptations, but "pseudo-adaptations," comparable to "pseudo-translations" in literature. Last, and this is a vital difference, drawn novels were not published separately, but rather as romance comics in a comic-book format in the front of a type of magazine in which readers did not expect to find comics. Until then, women's magazines included only a few small gag strips and an occasional short story or comics installment. But publications such as *Grand Hôtel* devoted most of their pages to the serialization of drawn novels. This new design involved a material difference in format, style, and retail and distribution systems, and also in the actual reading material. In magazines such as *Grand Hôtel* and *Nous Deux*, drawn novels did not occupy all the available space, and the juxtaposition of sometimes rather heterogeneous content had some effect on the way people read. The film photonovel became the heir of this (at times) surprising diversity.

Step 2: The Photonovel

Grand Hôtel and *Nous Deux*, and the drawn-novel formula more generally, were a hit, generating tremendous social excitement, despite the political and ideological resistance of both left-wing and right-wing forces. Neither the Communist Party nor the Catholic Church liked to see publications that exclusively focused on the individual "pursuit of happiness"; they accused them of promoting many moral and social evils (Giet 1997; on these institutions' lukewarm reuse of the genre to spread propaganda, see Bonifazio 2017). The success of both magazines immediately forced competitors to adopt their own strategies (the drawn-novel formula was copied or plagiarized almost overnight). At the same time, the drawn-novel craze was a menace to the other genres present in most women's magazines. The table of contents of the first issue of *Grand Hôtel* reflects the traditional potpourri of material, with a lot of attention given to domestic affairs and gossip (including the inevitable horoscope). But the popularity of the drawn novel led to the shrinking, and even elimination, of other sections.

In spite of the new genre's initial commercial victory, its position was anything but certain. In 1947, along with several competitors, *Grand Hôtel*—and later *Nous Deux*—launched another new formula, the photonovel, which presented itself as a drawn novel with pictures based on an original story (originality being a tricky and perhaps meaningless notion in the domain of popular fiction). First, *Il Mio Sogno* (My dream; the title was shortened to *Sogno*) on 8 May 1947 and soon afterward *Bolero-Film* on 25 May brought this new genre to Italian newsstands, and their triumph was as smashing as that of *Grand Hôtel* one year earlier.[4] Their French equivalents would have a similar impact (Faber, Minuit, and Takodjerad 2012).

From a visual and a narrative point of view, the first photonovels are not impressive. They miss the dynamic visual composition of the panels and the page layout of the drawn novel. The technical and financial restrictions that burden the photographic realization of many visual ideas tend to impoverish and stiffen the stories, which become sitting-room dramas, deprived of any graphic attractiveness—except that of the faces and bodies of the actors, which would soon be front and center in the new genre. For the publishers, photonovels were much cheaper and faster to produce than drawn novels, which were time-consuming (and thus expensive) and could be made only by well-trained craftsmen (mainly experienced artists working as illustrators for the magazine and book publishing industry). Given the ruthless competition in the field as well as difficulties in finding competent, punctual artists, the photonovel was a gift that they could not refuse.

But the question remains: what about the public? The instant success of the photonovel, which superseded the drawn novel in a few years, shows that the audience had no difficulties in making its choice. In 1950, *Grand Hôtel*, still the market leader among women's magazines, started including photonovels, and although it would continue to publish drawn novels for another decade, it was clear that the preferred format had changed. It is not clear why the audience readily accepted the photonovel without abandoning the drawn novel (although there must have been a link with the idea of realism, still the "cultural dominant" in the perception of photography as an indexical medium in those years). This realism, however, was not that of the stories, in spite of regular attempts to replace the overtly melodramatic story lines with more realistic content. *Bolero-Film*, for instance, had the reputation of being close to neorealism, whereas *Sogno*, in its first years, stuck more closely to the visual imaginary of Hollywood. The realism was that of faces, bodies, objects, and settings, all immediately recognizable and hence fundamental to building a relation of complicity between magazine, story, and reader, which was the key to success for all forms of popular fiction of the period.

Step 3: The Birth of the Film Photonovel

According to sociological surveys, photonovels were read by one out of three adults in Italy and France in the 1950s, and had a significant percentage of male readers, contrary to a deeply rooted misogynistic bias against the genre (for a survey of reading figures, see Giet 1997; Bravo 2003). Universally despised by left-wing and right-wing politicians and social activists, who boycotted the product for many years, the photonovel was considered the handmaiden of American soft power. It was scorned as a vicious and dangerous instrument of propaganda promoting the American way of life, instead of family values (on the right side of the political spectrum) or the necessity to commit oneself to social justice (on the left). The dream of individual happiness, which was the basic premise of all photonovels, was seen as essentially incompatible with the higher values of either family or society or both.

The resistance to the photonovel, a homegrown form of the European melodrama and installment-literature tradition, was contemporary with many other attempts to stop American culture at the border. For example, there were heated debates around the Blum-Byrnes agreements (1946), a series of French-American commercial agreements that aimed to eradicate France's war debt to America and to obtain new credits in exchange for opening France's markets to American products, especially films. In many French film histories, these agreements are still seen as a superlative trauma of blessed narcissism (for a nuanced and healthily nonpatriotic discussion, see Roger [2002] 2005). In France, the 1949 Family Protection Decree,[5] which controlled publications intended for the young and advocated the censorship of books that contravened morality, was used also to ban American comics in order to foster local comics production. Although the photonovel was not directly concerned with these polemics of production, the link to US culture in the genre is curious, perhaps a response to the influential anti-Americanist stances in western Europe at the beginning of the Cold War—also a culture war—which harmed the perception of the genre in French and Italian political and scholarly milieus. The general public, however, remained unaffected by these quarrels and continued to embrace romance and melodrama.

An important side effect of the photonovel vogue, which lasted until the full penetration of television into European households, was the emergence of a new genre, the film photonovel, which was a remediation of a genre almost as old as cinema itself: the film novel. Among film scholars, there is a consensus that the film novel—that is, a printed work that is the verbal double of an existing movie—is so diverse that it is impossible to reduce it to a single structure or model (Virmaux and Virmaux 1983; Faulkner 2008). Beginning in the 1910s, the story lines of serial films were simultaneously narrated in newspapers before being reprinted as books, an indicator of their popular success. An author such as Pierre Decourcelle, for instance, who serialized the US *Perils of Pauline* in 1915 and other material for the French newspaper *Le Matin* (Chabrier 2013; Letourneux 2015), pioneered this form of what we understand today as a typical case of transmedia storytelling in convergence culture (Jenkins 2006). The Edison Company–produced serial *What Happened to Mary*—based on stories that the all-purpose hack writer Robert Carlton Brown published, first as installments in *Ladies' World*, and then as a novel (1913)—is often considered the first real example of the complete cycle. The film-novel genre soon appeared in many different contexts, from one-shot modernist experiments to some of the crudest forms of commercial exploitation, the enormous variety making it impossible to attach a specific set of rules or features to the genre. In general, and with some inevitable simplification, the film novel field can be divided into three groups, which constantly intersect: the screenplay, sometimes illustrated; the illustrated or unillustrated short story or book-length novelization; and new forms of filmic retelling, sometimes freely departing from the original story. Modernist poetry, for example, has never ceased inventing new types of filmic retelling (McCabe 2005; Cohen 2016).

In this panorama, the film photonovel has a place of its own, but it is a paradoxical one. All film-novel types can be more or less linked with other genres that they update and redesign in reference to cinema. The screenplay (type 1) remakes the genre of the published play script. The novelization (type 2) is strongly influenced by romance and melodrama installment literature. The more experimental forms of narrating the movies (type 3) are symbiotic with other ongoing experiments in poetry. Unlike other film-novel types, the film photonovel is a somewhat extreme example of an apparently slavish remediation, for it seems to imitate (almost as an exact replica) uncritically the language of the photonovel at a time when print was the dominant cultural medium for popular fiction. This impression, however, is deceptive, for even though the film photonovel seems to completely align with specific features of both the film novel and the photonovel, this process of "changing partners" is not neutral or transparent. In practice, there are essential differences between a photonovel and a film photonovel, and the reuse of the former by the latter is much more than a case of passive or purely commercially motivated imitation. What is clear is that there is a strong appropriation of the photonovel by the film novel, whose outcome produces the hybrid form of the film photonovel.

Are Film Photonovels (Just) Photonovels?

A first misunderstanding, easy to discard, is related to the images themselves. The specific quality of a film photonovel has little to do with the fact that it reuses pictures of a real movie, whether film stills or set pictures (a dichotomy addressed later in this chapter and in chapter 4). Other types of film novels already did so, sometimes with similar results, such as the series that illustrated each shot or dialogue line with a single image. These series existed in all countries with a strong culture of film production. In Italy between 1936 and 1946, the *Cinevita* weekly series published film novels that reproduced the complete story of a film with stills, shot after shot, that contained the complete dialogue of the movie. The formula was repeated around 1950 in *Foto Film* magazine, which later shifted to "real" film photonovels. In 1974, Richard J. Anobile's Film Classics Library published a small number of volumes that follow the same principle: "Over 1.000 frame blow-ups. Every scene. Every Word of Dialogue," claims the back cover of these books, which consist of approximately 250 pages each.[6]

In France, Balland published a few film novels in its La Bibliothèque des classiques du cinéma (Classic movies library) series in 1978.[7]

These series can be defined as trade versions of the cinephile approach to the film novel, a genre generally associated with a lowbrow audience. The film photonovel, however, does not retell the story simply with the help of a sequence of captioned images; it does so by merging this format with the basic features of the photonovel—for instance, text balloons or melodramatic inspiration, which were not used in the aforementioned film-novel series, as they depended primarily on filmic illustrations. The similarities between the photonovel and film photonovel help demonstrate why a work such as Anobile's *Stagecoach* is less a film photonovel than a film novel. Other examples of this can be seen in the publications of *Foto Film*, the Classics Library, or La Bibliothèque des classiques du cinema, which lack the creative tension that the film photonovel both copied and rejected (for a typical example from this period, see fig. 2.2).

The true film photonovel developed when captioned visual film novels morphed into a format that completely merged texts (speech, thought balloons, and narrative voice-overs) and images. Although there is no clear-cut transition from the old to the new model, it is generally accepted that it originated with the magazine *Super Cinema*, which proposed such an integration (sixteen pages, one hundred fifty images, thirty lire) in its adaptation of *Il Brigante Musolino* (1950, Mario Camerini; released in the United States as *Outlaw Girl*). The shift from narrated film novel or captioned visual film novel to film photonovel was the direct result of the triumph of the photonovel, which had dramatically redefined the field since its appearance in 1947 (it was also in 1950 that *Grand Hôtel* started incorporating photonovels next to its drawn novels). In the following years, many film photonovel magazines emerged and then rapidly disappeared before new publishers started dominating the field: Victory, which claimed to invent the genre with the publication, in November 1952, of the magazine *I grandi fotoromanzi d'amore*; La Lanterna Magica, supported by the film producer Dino De Laurentiis (*Cineromanzo Gigante* and *Cineromanzo per tutti*); Franco Bozzesi (via *Star Cineromanzo Gigante* and *I Vostri Film*); and some years later, after the collapse of most other series, Edoardo Rovelli (the first to publish in color, with *Roman Film Color*).

But what does it mean to stress the influence—an old-fashioned word, but very pertinent in this context—of the photonovel on the film photonovel? This question is the key component that differentiates the hybrid genre from previous forms of film novels.

First, the film photonovel reuses the traditional page layout of a photonovel, which prototypically comes down to a three-by-two grid. A page

White Scout: Naw—he's a Cheyenne. They hate Apaches worse than we do.

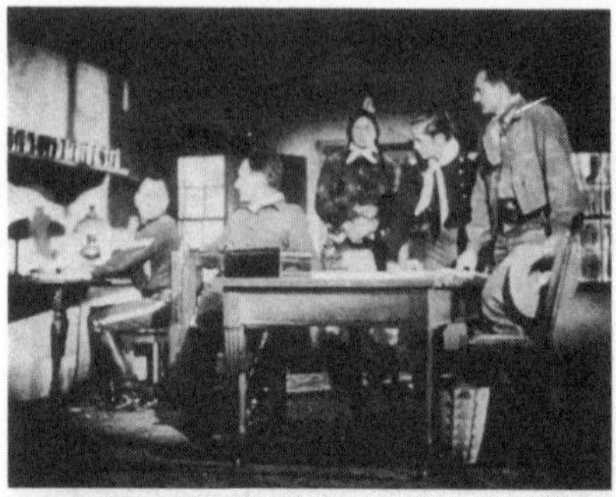

Capt. Sickels: Clear the wire to Lordsburg.

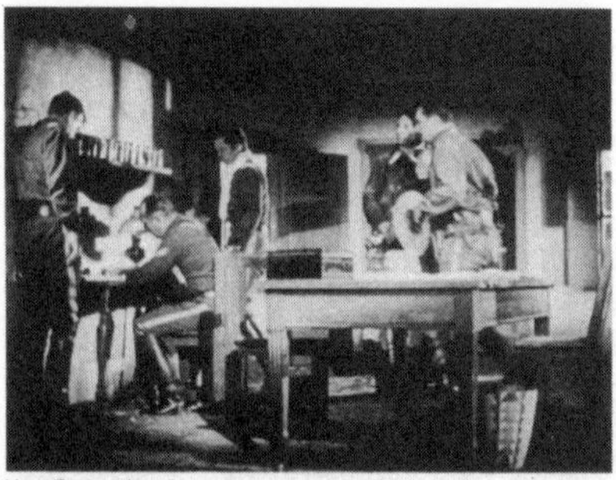

Non-Com: That's Lordsburg now, sir. They seem to have something very urgent to tell you, sir.
Capt. Sickels: Well—what's wrong?

Non-Com: The line went dead, sir.
Capt. Sickels: What've you got there?

Non-Com: Only the first word, sir.

Capt. Sickels: Geronimo!

11

FIGURE 2.1. Stagecoach *(*Stagecoach, *1939, John Ford), Film Classics Library, 1975, p. 11.*

FIGURE 2.2. *"Cuori vagabondi,"* Il Mio Sogno, *2 May 1948, p. 3.*

is divided into three rows (in principle, all with the same width and the same height), each having two pictures (which can be of the same size but can also present small differences in width). Moreover, the use of this page layout reinforces a specific type of word-image relationship. Captions and speech balloons are normally present inside the frame, and narrative captions penetrate the space of the photographs. Text is almost always present. The photonovel strongly avoids "mute" images, despite the technical and aesthetic difference resulting from adding words to images. These works may frequently have text-only panels, but few images are without text. The photonovel is unquestionably a talkative genre, even if there was, from the very start, an attempt to downsize the number of words, both inside the frames and on the page. This layout system was not invented from scratch, since the first photonovels were heavily influenced by, and yet struggled against, the richer and more elastic page layout of the drawn novel. But by the time the film photonovel appeared, the grid system had become a well-established norm. The first iterations of the new genre could thus rely on a functional model. To a certain extent, the film photonovel proved more conservative than its model, since the latter frequently tried to escape the stereotypical three-by-two grid. The film photonovel, by contrast, seemed much more accepting of this kind of layout: unlike the photonovel, known for its variations (superficial though they may have been), the film photonovel was much more willing to unquestioningly use the three-by-two grid. As will be discussed later, the film photonovel's variations on the basic system were, however, always pertinent.

A second major characteristic borrowed from the photonovel exceeds both genre and medium structures. Like photonovels, film photonovels tend to be melodramas. The notion of the melodrama, whose function in first-age cinema can hardly be overestimated, has been intensely discussed in literary and cultural studies. It is both a transhistorical and a highly local phenomenon. Peter Brooks's study of the melodramatic imagination demonstrates the usefulness of distinguishing between the melodramatic as a universal mode and historically rooted forms of melodrama, such as the nineteenth-century, post–French Revolution melodrama (Brooks [1976] 1995). For the corpus analyzed here, scholars stress the need to separate American and Italian forms of melodrama: the former sharply focuses on individual psychological dramas of the nuclear family, while the latter insists on the social dimension of the narrative (Morreale 2011). In the photonovel, the melodramatic aspects involve the story first and the visual language second, chiefly the pose and the aesthetics of the *tableau vivant*. From a narrative point of view, the photonovel is not necessarily sensational, but it is always exaggerated; some of its key themes are the misadventures and persecution of innocent love, its eventual punishment or redemption, misunderstandings due to mistaken identities, and the restoration of traditional family values. Visually, typical pictures in photonovel melodramas capture not a movement in action, but a symbolic—often aggrandized and thus highly "readable"—pose; and the same applies to the sequential arrangements of its images, which do not reproduce the successive moments of such an action but rather a set of variations on the same pose. The symbolic "violence" exerted by the old photonovel format on the film photonovel is crystal clear. Whatever the genre or ideological sensibility that the stories sustain, they are systematically reframed or even rewritten in such a way that the film photonovel version of the film becomes a melodrama—or at least reinforces the film's melodramatic dimension. This rewriting obeys clearly observable patterns, which are examined in chapter 3.

A third major characteristic of the film photonovel has to do with the publication format, which was always that of a magazine on sale at newsstands.[8] Some, often heavily illustrated film-novel types were published in journals and magazines, yet never in ways that closely resembled the visual and editorial properties of the photonovel magazines. In some cases, these were not initially produced by companies with a strong photonovel line but were taken over by the latter. Once the film-photonovel format had become commercially successful, it was rapidly copied by photonovel publishers—a strategic move not unlike the adoption of the photonovel formula by the major drawn-novel magazines such as *Grand Hôtel* and *Nous Deux*.

There were two major types of film-photonovel magazines: those exclusively devoted to the genre, and those that mixed it with comparable genres such as the photonovel, the drawn novel, and one or more variations on the film novel. What matters here is less the global correspondence between these two types than the impact that each magazine tried to make in the larger field. Magazines sold not because they were more or less exclusively devoted to film photonovels—to a certain extent, all of them were—but because the public thought that they offered something their competitors could not. Value for money was the key, as is often the case in popular fiction. Hence the importance of aspects such as the price of the magazine (always visibly announced on the front cover); the number of pages (the more the better); the presence of celebrities (publicized on the back or front cover—in neither case was it necessary for the movie star to actually play a part in the film photonovel itself);[9] the periodicity (monthly magazines had more aura than weeklies); the presence or absence of full-color images inside the magazine (in these years, still an exception in photonovel production); and the prestige of the adapted movies, although this was a less decisive feature than it may initially appear (most magazines were open to all kinds of movies, not only because there were so many of them but also because the target audience was not cinephiles).

The distinction between "pure" and "mixed" film photo-magazines was not static, and the relationship between the two types changed over time, although not always along the same curve. Since the film photonovel can be defined as an episode in the longer history of the film novel—an episode whose birth and death can be explained by the pressure of the photonovel as a temporarily dominant medium in the broader field of popular magazine culture—it is not surprising that some film-photonovel magazines, like film-novel magazines, were created from scratch, while others appeared to remediate existing publications. The former were typically the result of the discovery of a new niche in the market. The latter, which appeared somewhat later but often lasted longer, exemplified established players' reactions to newcomers in the field. In Italy, where the film photonovel was launched, the most important examples of the new medium clearly belonged to the first category. In France, where the film photonovel started somewhat later, famous, highly successful examples of older film-novel or photonovel magazines decided to shift to the film-photonovel formula. At the end of the cycle, that history reversed itself: magazines that were "pure" film photonovels tended to disappear, whereas "mixed" forms that had progressively favored the film-photonovel formula returned to their old formulas, whether photonovels or film novels (blended with a variety of movie magazines).

The most striking example of the rise and fall of a film-photonovel magazine was perhaps *Mon Film* (My movie), the leading French film magazine published between 1924 and 1967 (with a brief hiatus from 1938 to 1946).[10] Its concept was as simple as it was efficient: each weekly issue offered a brief novelization of a movie, which was accompanied by information about its main actors. Thanks to its small but visually attractive format—an illustrated cover in addition to sixteen very small pages containing approximately ten images from the movie[11]—*Mon Film* could be seen as the popular short-cut version of such longer novelization series (also popular in the 1920s and 1930s) as the weekly Cinéma-Bibliothèque (Film library) volumes, published by Jules Tallandier, a company that specialized in popular and pulp fiction (Letourneux and Mollier 2011). *Mon Film* was published as a weekly until February 1959, when it absorbed another lowbrow magazine, *Le Film Complet* (The complete movie), and became a monthly publication. From 1957 on, it published special issues of film photonovels, which soon adopted a larger format, close to that of the A4 format (8.27 in × 11.7 in.) of *Mon Film*. These special issues first appeared under a separate series title, *Mon Film Spécial* (My special movie). After the merger with *Le Film complet*, *Mon Film* completely abandoned its old film-novel formula. Starting in 1960, the film photonovels were no longer released under the title *Mon Film Spécial* but under the initial title of the publication, *Mon Film*. The series catalogue includes 112 film photonovels, all based on French movies, an unusual policy in the film-photonovel business, which tended to ignore national, linguistic, and genre frontiers. This "nationalization" was, however, not the most interesting feature of *Mon Film*, which radically adopted a medium-specific layout style, as will be studied in more detail in what follows.

The release of the film photonovels in a singular publication format—as a weekly, semimonthly, or monthly magazine on sale at newsstands—had a tremendous impact on its form as well as its reception. This was demonstrated most visibly in the adoption of a strong house style in a magazine's editorial formula and in its stories. Each magazine—and we should note the merciless competition between dozens of similar magazines fighting for the customer's attention in the congested newsstands—proposed a "unique" mix of textual and paratextual elements. Magazine X combined film photonovels and gossip sections with a chaste pinup picture as the centerfold and a celebrity interview, whereas magazine Y used as its unique selling point a combination of film photonovels, photonovels, short stories, and reportage, always in a recognizable and repeated order. Generally speaking, the more serious a publication tried to be, the more space it devoted to film photonovels. In addition to maverick productions that tended to foreground other material—announcements, short stories, comics, gossip sections, horoscopes, and the like—*Nous Deux Film*, the major French competitor of *Mon Film* and, in principle, a rather upscale magazine in this domain, had a similar policy of devoting more space to film photonovels. Regarding the stories themselves—more precisely, the material presentation of these stories, since not all magazines specialized in a certain type of cinema—at least in the first years, most magazines published "everything," that is, film photonovels of all films whose adaptation rights could be obtained.[12]

Each publication proposed its own mix of comparable ingredients, and the sequence of these items was unmistakably structured to function as the paper equivalent of a night at the movies, whose audiences likewise knew what to expect from the theatrical experience (Morreale 2007a, 153). Theater owners, in that regard, were an extension of the film companies: when going to a certain theater—which generally screened movies from a given company and showed in order all the filmic types that accompanied the A movie (cartoons, newsreels, advertisements, a B movie, tourism promotions)—the public had a clear idea of what it would get for its money, and film photonovels were able to promise a similar experience.

Moreover, the material presentation of film photonovels always matched the "image" of the magazine. The house style of each governed page layout, lettering techniques, the use of a certain type of narrative voice-over, the number of pages, the choice between film stills and set pictures, and the relationships between sections of the magazine. This style was imposed on all the films adapted by the magazine's creative team. Let us examine, for instance, the practice of *Mon Film*. The magazine published only French film photonovels, without making any distinction between genres, styles, companies, or directors, and it had a direct relationship with the film-novel tradition. It also had a signature look due to the combination of set pictures (never film stills), a rigid but clear layout (which scrupulously respected the three-by-two grid), and a perhaps somewhat artificial but very readable technique for the insertion of captions and speech balloons (black letters on white surfaces glued on the pictures). Finally, *Mon Film* had a recognizable peritextual policy: comparatively few non-film-photonovel pages, less space devoted to gossip than to short photonovel stories, and a publicity section with a recurrent focus on advertisements for breast-enhancing products. The pursuit of such an image was undoubtedly a top priority for all magazines of this type.

Why Film Photonovels Are Not Photonovels

There are important differences between the film photonovel and the photonovel. Three elements stand out. First, film photonovels were almost always published as complete stories. The number of stories published in installments was low, and that formula rapidly disappeared. The reason for this choice, unusual in the field of popular fiction for women, which had long been dominated by serial forms of melodrama, is easy to understand. Film photonovels were always published after the film's release, sometimes many years later, so the genre addresses a knowing audience, that is, an audience that has had the opportunity to see the movie or to become familiar with the story, including its denouement, via reviews or word of mouth. Serialization would have been pointless. Also, the publication of complete stories may have been perceived as a form of status building, since it distinguished the film photonovel from its younger brother, the methodically serialized photonovel.

A small digression on sales prices is necessary here. Status in the context of popular fiction is always related to financial and economic issues, and this starts with the price of the magazine. Here the difference between Italy and France is noteworthy. In both countries, the visual and editorial context of the film photonovel was undoubtedly that of the photonovel at the newsstand, but in neither country did this family resemblance translate to similarity in pricing. On the contrary, the average price of a photonovel magazine in Italy in 1955 was approximately 30 to 40 lire,[13] but the average price of a film photonovel was noticeably more expensive, although some maverick publishers were not afraid of releasing material of inferior quality for a much lower price: compare, for example, the 100–150 lire price range of the market leaders with the 30 lire cost, in 1956, of the *Cineromanzo economico* series published by Gioggi. In a memoir of his discovery of cinema, the film director and passionate film-photonovel reader Gianni Amelio extensively comments on this aspect (Amelio 2007). His remarks make clear that the Italian film photonovel, at least in its first period, did not address the same broad audience as the photonovel, whose extremely low prices had completely reshuffled the world of women's magazines. Together with the changes in film culture taking place at that time, namely, the shift from a popular and lowbrow cinema to a more sophisticated take on film as art, this financial threshold has to be taken into account when discussing the rapid downfall of the film photonovel in Italy.

In France, the price gap was smaller, yet not insignificant. In 1957, when the film photonovel was firmly established in the market, a single issue of the photonovel magazine *Nous Deux* cost 50 francs, while issues of film photonovels were sold at 40 francs (*Les Films pour vous* magazine, published by La Torraccia), 50 francs (*Ciné-Révélation*, published by Editor), 60 francs (*Hebdo Roman*, published by Victory), 70 francs (*Roman Film d'amour et d'aventures*, La Torraccia), or 80 francs (*Nous Deux Films*, Les Éditions mondiales). The most expensive film-photo magazine in the early years was *Roman Film Color* (launched by La Torraccia in 1958), the first one to be published in color. The most obvious case in point here is the price setting of Les Éditions mondiales—the publisher of the leading photonovel magazine, *Nous Deux*—which ran several film-photonovel magazines in parallel with its usual products. The film-photonovel series of the group were only slightly more expensive than its main photonovel magazine. In later years, prices rose from 80 to 100 francs after the 1960 monetary reform that converted 100 old francs to 1 new franc, but these were years with a rather high inflation rate.

A second difference between the two media under scrutiny is the systematic anonymity of the makers of film photonovels, whose names never appear in print as the "authors" of the works. This kind of anonymity did not apply to the photonovel. Even if some photonovels remained unsigned or were signed with pseudonyms (in popular genre fiction, these practices are still common), most of the time there was a double signature: that of the "author" (often the whole film production team: director, photographer, scriptwriter, and actor) and that of the "producer" (specialized companies that worked as subcontractors for photonovel magazines). The more prestigious the photonovel, the more detailed the credits.[14] At first sight, this lack of authorial identification in the film photonovel—a general practice with only a few, generally bizarre exceptions[15]—may seem astonishing, for it contradicts the idea of cultural "upgrading" resulting from the shift from serial publication to the complete-story format. What it reveals, though, is that the prestige of the work belonged exclusively to the adapted source (the film), not the adapting target (the film photonovel). Moreover, it diminishes the importance of the actual creator, accentuating instead the role of the producer—in this case, the magazine, which appears as the real author of the work. The general observations on the importance of the magazine's house style pointed in this direction. The close reading of some of the formal narrative properties of the film photonovel in the next chapter will reinforce this interpretation.

Genre and readership constitute a third crucial difference between the photonovel and film photonovel. Although the latter functioned commercially under the wings of the former, the intended audience was not completely the same—if the audiences had been the same, the selection of the adapted movies would have taken into account the supposed preferences of the allegedly female public of the photonovel, which was definitely not the case. At least in its golden age (1954–1964), the film photonovel can be described as relatively "genre blind," for the films that were turned into "films in print" belonged to all genres: thrillers, weepies, swashbuckling adventures, psychological dramas, romantic comedies, and existentialist avant-garde films. It was only with the vanishing of the classic film photonovel after 1965 that there was a radical reorientation toward typically male genres such as westerns, horror, science fiction, and pornography. Although not much is known about the readership of film photonovels—we only have a small number of oral history testimonies at our disposal, which do not easily allow for generalization—it seems reasonable to suppose that the readers were both more diverse and more specialized than photonovel lovers, hence the differences between the two media. It is not possible to claim that all photonovel readers also bought film photonovels; the differences in print runs suggest that only some of them did. Nor is it evident that film-photonovel lovers were also interested in photonovels; some of the few direct testimonies that we have suggest that their focus was exclusively on cinema.

Reading or Looking At?

As mentioned, the film photonovel started in Italy around 1954[16] and moved to France when the Italian public's interest started to diminish. The genre collapsed suddenly in Italy after just two or three years and survived only within narrowly defined "genre fiction" frontiers (science fiction, horror, westerns, and porn). The evolution in France was somewhat slower, in several regards. Although the film photonovel started later in France, it survived longer, extending into the mid-1960s. By then, the move toward genre film photonovels was irreversible. This "degraded" version of the genre lasted well into the late seventies, when videocassettes took over and sales of film photonovels moved to sex shops. The difference between Italy and France demonstrates the reception and, thus, the very raison d'être of the film photonovel as well as its place in the cinematographic culture of its time.

Film was ubiquitous, and moviegoing attained its highest postwar figures during the 1950s. In Italy, the peak year was 1955, with 825 million tickets sold at the box office; in France, the peak year was 1957, with 411.6 million tickets sold. At the time, theaters were beacons of the visual imaginary of the film industry: posters, marquee paintings, picture displays in lobbies, and windows on the street. In addition, the general press and countless professional and fan magazines brought information about movies to all homes. Many specialized activities around cinema bolstered the core of the popular-film experience: for instance, the trade in movie star photos or in official or improvised celebrity pictures, well documented in the Italian context by Giovanni Fiorentino (1995) in his study of the on-location shooting of *Pane, Amore e . . .* (*Scandal in Sorrento*, Dino Risi), the 1955 "trequel" to *Pane, amore e fantasia* (1953) and *Pane, amore e gelosia* (1954), both directed by Luigi Comencini. The shooting of this film, which costars the film director Vittorio De Sica, who was also a brilliant actor, and Sophia Loren,[17] already the greatest Italian movie star of the decade (and those to come, after a not-very-successful American intermezzo), generated a remarkable number of vernacular souvenir photographs—some made by passers-by, others taken by local photographers catering to tourists—which completed and diversified the equally important picture business orchestrated by the producers.

At the same time, film culture remained strangely nonvisual, that is, purely verbal. Celebrity and publicity pictures flooded the market, but most articles and other writings on film remained mostly imageless. Even specialized magazines included few if any illustrations, and in the years before television (which in the beginning did not schedule many movies), videocassettes, DVDs, Blu-ray discs, and streaming, chances to see film images outside the generally short-run, ephemeral, and sometimes inaccessible theatrical screenings were rather slim. Films rapidly moved from one exhibition venue to another and then "vanished." The film photonovel was the perfect solution for all those eager to keep a material trace of the movies they had seen or wanted to see, and it enabled a theoretically endless, infinitely repeatable film experience. Most testimonies of those who read and purchased film photonovels acknowledge that the photonovels mainly performed that memory function, which was partially a vicarious experience. In addition, film photonovels allowed people to "remember" movies that they had not yet seen except in their imaginations. Film lovers undoubtedly considered the film photonovel an appropriate way to stay in touch with the moviegoing experience.

The genre had other advantages as well. It facilitated the transformation of a collective experience, since private viewings of films were practically unheard of, into a highly subjective and personal reading experience, as we can deduce from the wholesale lots found on eBay, at garage sales, and so on. Often these lots are heterogeneous, reflecting the personal taste of a previous owner who did not collect the complete series of certain magazines but only bought, for instance, film photonovels starring a particular movie star or adapting a specific movie genre. Moreover, the film photonovel was open to uses other than reading, as indicated by the following announcement, printed on the front cover of a (rare) Spanish adaptation of Fellini's *Nights of Cabiria* (1957): "Recorte y separe esta hoja. Con la fotografía que figura al dorso y colocándola en un marco, se obtendrá un bello cuadrito" (Cut out this page. Put the picture at the back in a frame, and you will obtain a nice poster).[18] In other words, this material was not for reading alone. It was also for looking at, and the lack of certain pages in the magazines in some archives (or offered for sale) implies that this function was far from being a minor detail: centerfold images or back covers featuring a full-color picture of a movie star are frequently missing (in some cases, readers even cut out single panels). Apparently, film photonovels were purchased to be transformed into private or domestic icons.

Finally, as a testament to the porosity of the frontiers between the worlds of the photonovel and the cinema, the photonovel in Italy was for many years a springboard to a more lucrative career in the film business. A plethora of movie superstars, such as Sophia Loren and Gina Lollobrigida, started as photonovel starlets, after which they enjoyed exceptional popularity in the field before making it in Cinecittà and Hollywood. Film photonovels did not have that same function, but they could be the only way to get recent full-color pictures of celebrities who had changed their names and no longer wanted to be reminded of their previous and less glamorous life in the photonovel industry.[19]

Producing the Film Photonovel: Between Movies and Magazines

The film photonovel world consisted of readers but also entrepreneurs, whether they were new to the business or experienced publishers eager to diversify their photonovel catalogues. Additionally, the very existence of the genre was unthinkable without the active or passive support of film producers and distributors. Although not much is known regarding the legal aspects of the film photonovel trade, some of them have been reported. In Italy, copyright and authorization issues were subcontracted to those who made the film photonovels (Mercuri 2007; for some legal issues, see Morreale 2007c), and in France, the film photonovel adaptations were mentioned in some contracts between film producers and directors.[20] The Italian subcontracting policy—meaning that contacts with the film producer or distributor were managed not by the magazine publisher but by the freelancer who physically made the film photonovel—did not rely on a fixed legal framework. In many cases, everything seems to have been settled by personal contacts, and improvisation must have been prevalent. The French inclusion of the film-photonovel version as part of a package of derived rights, or more precisely, as the only derived right that belonged to the director (all the others belonging to the producer), meant at least two things: first, that the practice was sufficiently established to be integrated in standard legal contracts; second, that the financial and other benefits of film-photonovel adaptations were probably not large enough to be of any interest to the producer or the distributor. Thus, it seems clear that the whole film-photonovel trade was only somewhat modestly profitable. Otherwise, producers and distributors would certainly have tried to get tighter control of it. As Michele Mercuri subtly specifies, the film photonovel certainly helped some people make some money, but nobody struck it rich (Mercuri 2007).

In hindsight, and in the absence of more firsthand testimonies, it is difficult to make an accurate analysis of the film-photonovel producers' policy. The poor print quality of some film photonovels should leave us dismayed. The resolution of the images is sometimes so bad that one can hardly recognize the original picture or tell whether the image is a photograph or a drawing. The blurriness of the image was not a problem for adaptations of B movies or for those published in semilegal magazines, but it did affect photos taken from big-budget Hollywood productions.

FIGURE 2.3. *"La Fureur de vivre" (*Rebel Without a Cause*, 1955, Nicholas Ray),* Star Ciné Roman*, 1 November 1958, p. 25.*

A typical example is the movie that made James Dean a star: *Rebel Without a Cause* (Nicholas Ray, 1955), published as a film photonovel in Italian in *Star Cineromanzo Gigante* and reissued in French in *Star Ciné Roman*, each by Bozzesi, generally considered one of the best publishers in the field (fig. 2.3). The deficient image quality was probably due to technical difficulties with the treatment of color and wide-screen technology (a comparison with two other James Dean movies, *East of Eden* and *Giant*, shows some increase in quality, but the overall quality of the new film photonovels was still subpar).

Similar observations could be made concerning the adaptation techniques themselves. Apparently there was little or no control regarding how the pictures were selected, cropped, edited, and systematically used in melodramatic plots, a common rewriting mechanism. Even though melodrama was an important part of film culture in the 1950s, not all films were marketed as melodramas; but adaptations nonetheless tended to incorporate melodramatic elements. Yet despite the miserable visual quality, the whimsical narratives, and the ideological reframing of story material, most film companies did not oppose the regular, though unsystematic, reworking of their movies into film photonovels. Even companies considered hostile to these adaptations did not totally reject them, probably because local distributors and company representatives had some degree of autonomy. Emiliano Morreale (2007a, 48) repeatedly emphasizes the unwillingness of Fox and Universal to grant film-photonovel authorizations, although a closer look at the backlists of some magazines reveals that even these companies occasionally agreed to a film photonovel adaptation.[21]

Another complicating factor was that film photonovels generally appeared after the films had finished their commercial circulation. Some adaptations were published soon after the theatrical release of the adapted film, but the temporal distance between both moments was not negligible—in many cases it was substantial, with certain series publishing adaptations of films that were more than five years old—so it is reasonable to assume that most works offered for sale in the magazines could no longer be seen in theaters. Some magazines with good contacts in the film business could release a film-photonovel version almost immediately after the theatrical release of popular movies (in Italy, the Lanterna Magica publications, supported by producer Dino De Laurentiis; in France, *Mon Film*). Less established magazines were often obliged to fill their weekly issues with lesser-known and, above all, older material. The film photonovel thus gave new life to some Italo-German productions of the fascist era. This fact does not mean that certain publishers could always afford recent, attractive adaptations while others had to recycle old and often suspect material. With the exception of *Mon Film*, no series had homogeneous catalogues of up-to-date movies (and even *Mon Film* was open to all genres covered by mainstream French film production in these years).

The temporal gap between original movie and adaptation in print helps account for certain technical flaws of the film photonovel as a print product. If the magazine could not use pictures taken on set, it had to wait for the copies of the film to be returned to the distributor's office, where one could then take photos of film stills—and the copies of some films were corroded by countless screenings. The time lag between a movie and its film photonovel also implies that the adaptation had low publicity value for the film itself, unlike many novelizations, whose publication dates were often much closer to those of the theatrical release of the films. But film photonovels were nonetheless a key tool in celebrity culture and part of the endless promotion machine of the film industry. Readers may have bought film photonovels to experience a known or unknown movie, but also to possess the image of an idol, almost like a fetish object, and in the studio system, these idols never stopped reappearing in "new" vehicles.[22] Film companies ardently welcomed the survival of old movies featuring the stars of movies to come. From that point of view, even film photonovels of films no longer in circulation could still function as publicity for upcoming movies with the same stars.

The Death of the Film Photonovel

All these elements might make the relatively sudden disappearance of the film photonovel, first in Italy and then in France, a mystery. Readers purchased huge numbers of these magazines, and producers and distributors did not feel threatened by their existence. So how to explain the rapid decline in interest in the genre and its eventual move to covering substandard genre films? (The number of spaghetti westerns mechanically translated into film photonovels from the mid-1960s was mind-numbing.) The decline and fall of the film photonovel is a complex question that remains unanswered. In the available testimonies and analyses, two elements are generally stressed: the lasting impact of the photonovel, on the hand, and the changes in film culture, on the other. These two elements are inextricably linked.

As we have seen, the negative impact of the close relationship between film photonovels and photonovels was apparent. The latter was never taken seriously—except by its numerous readers, but they were culturally and socially suspect, even crudely scorned (the voice of supposedly semiliterate women was—and still is—difficult to hear, even in so-called progressive circles). The film photonovel was even more despised (hence Morreale's shocking label of "lumpen photonovel"). The question remains what these arguments mean for the case of the photonovel version of a popular movie, for instance, a tearjerker by Matarazzo (an extremely productive director who was the king of weepy Italian melodrama in the first half of the 1950s; see *Cinegrafie* 2007). This kind of cinema lent itself perfectly to adaptation by a film photonovel, since several of Matarazzo's melodramas were adaptations of the photonovel world. The two movies that signified his return to the Italian scene, the 1949 *Catene* and the 1950 *Tormento*, were filmic reinterpretations of melodramas that had been "tested" in the photonovel business before their adaptations to the screen. "Catene" and "Tormento" were the titles of the first two photonovels published by Bolero-Film in 1947, and although Matarazzo did not adapt the plots of these works, the intertextual allusions would have been clear to Italian audiences.[23] Moreover, as Emiliano Morreale has aptly pointed out, the posters for Matarazzo films highlighted the link with the film novel by adding captions to their central image so that it resembled a quotation from a photonovel—a nonexistent photonovel, but the drawn-novel and photonovel readers did not care about these pseudo-references (Morreale 2011).

The film photonovel and the photonovel are related by their visual, narrative, and ideological styles. It is therefore a logical extension to posit that at least in Italy, the sudden downfall of the film photonovel resulted from some fundamental changes in the film industry. The fading out of popular cinema—as epitomized by the Matarazzo films as well as by several examples of Hollywood productions, and their rapid replacement by a totally new form of auteur cinema, director-centered and targeting a young, urban, better-educated audience—provoked a split between high-brow adapted films and the language of the lowbrow adapting medium (Morreale 2007d). When film became more than entertainment and new forms of highbrow cinephilia appeared (De Baecque [2002] 2013), the "vulgar" film photonovel was no longer used as the privileged double or substitute for "enlightened" moviegoing. To put it more simply: the "old" audience consumed the photonovel, which was no longer in touch with the types of films being made by the younger generation, and the "new" audience strongly rejected the photonovel and thus also the film photonovel as disgraceful remnants of the past. The films of Antonioni, Fellini, Visconti, Rossellini, and De Sica, for example, were adapted as film photonovels, but their followers, the new movie audience, had already begun to turn to other types of film in print, mainly the published screenplay.

The same phenomenon could be observed in France, although in a softened fashion. As mentioned, the film photonovel in France was initially an Italian import (the crisis in their domestic market pushed Italian publishers to start printing in French in an effort to expand); the critical and aesthetic changes in film culture, however, were not the same as in Italy. In France, the fault line was not so much a divide between popular cinema and art-house cinema as one between old and new production forms of art cinema: the former were referred to as "French quality" movies, often ambitious adaptations of literary masterpieces whose key agent was not the scriptwriter; the latter put an absolute emphasis on the director as sole creator of the worldview communicated by the movie. Apparently, film photonovels in this context were less contaminated by the intimate relationship between sentimental, popular cinema and photonovels, as shown by the use of the film photonovel in popular publishing venues. In 1969, for example, Raoul Coutard, Jean-Luc Godard's photographer, published a film-photonovel version of *Breathless* (1960) in the Parisian newspaper *Le Parisien libéré* (see Calafat and Deschamps 2017 and Pinchon and Calafat 2018 for the complete story of Godard's use of the photonovel format and circuit). Younger and more intellectual French audiences did not feel the same resentment for the family resemblance between the photonovel and the film photonovel as was felt in Italy. But the declining global quality of the photonovel in the 1960s had an inevitable impact on the film photonovel. The initial acceptance of the format, which explains the strong involvement of specialized photonovel publishers in the film-photonovel trade, weeklies and monthlies alike, could not be maintained without consequences, and just as in Italy, the film photonovel survived only in certain niches, some of them closer to the sex shop than to the newsstand.

As this overview suggests, the disappearance of the film photonovel was not the product of a single event, but a transformation through a series of steps. First, the genre lost the capacity to absorb virtually everything that appeared on screen. After having been used as a genre-insensitive vehicle, the film photonovel was reduced to serving three or four niche markets, often with bad reputations.

A second, indirectly visible but no less significant change was the internal reconversion of certain film-photonovel magazines. Instead of vanishing from the market, they replaced the proper film-photonovel section with something else—for instance, a photonovel or an illustrated short story novelization.[24] It should be kept in mind that photonovel producers preferred to maintain a lasting confusion between the film photonovel and the filmic photonovel. Just like drawn novels, which were implicitly marketed as filmic adaptations, countless photonovels were deliberately published with deceiving titles such as "photo film," "photo movie," "film adventure," and so forth, and the generic confusion was not always easy to untangle. A comparable yet culturally more significant change was the reaction of the film photonovel to the internal transformation of the second of its mother genres: the film novel. Indeed, the collapse of the film photonovel not only made room for a return of the photonovel but also spurred a sudden revival of the film novel. During the early sixties, several New Wave directors—in France, examples included Jean-Luc Godard, Alain Resnais, and Marguerite Duras—started developing experimental types of film novels whose distinctive feature was their relative autonomy from the adapted movie. *Last Year at Marienbad* (Robbe-Grillet [1961] 1962) is no longer read just as the book version of the eponymous movie by Alain Resnais (1961); it is, above all, an independent work of its screenwriter, a work that has the ambition to reinvent the somewhat fossilized genre of the film novel. The success of these books was, however, short-lived, mainly because the writers involved, such as Alain Robbe-Grillet and Marguerite Duras, preferred to challenge the old divide between film and literature in other ways. Instead of writing "literary" screenplays, they started making movies themselves, and although Robbe-Grillet continued to publish film novels, the genre as such was not institutionalized in the avant-garde segment of literary production.

The third and last episode in the fading out of the film photonovel was the redefinition of the remaining works within narrow genre boundaries of fiction (horror, science fiction, war, crime, and porn), accompanied by a similarly gendered repositioning of the audience. Whatever conclusions are to be made from this evolution, which increased the film photonovel's marginalization as a self-fulfilling prophecy, the push to redefine the position and status of the photonovel represented a crisis in the period. But unlike the film photonovel, the photonovel not only survived in the margins, but also managed to reinvent itself, at least for some years, in formats that the film photonovel could not traverse: parody and political satire; modernization of the romance universe through a partnership with television and celebrity culture; and new types of middlebrow literary adaptations. Regardless of the visual and narrative qualities that we might attribute to these works, they ultimately suggest a cultural dynamism that the film photonovel was no longer capable of maintaining.

A Problem-Solving Machine

Probably one of the most salient features of the film photonovel is related to the constraints that both limited and enabled its production. Before examining the chief problems and opportunities that characterized the medium, it is useful to list these constraints briefly, since they represent both a summary of some essential observations disclosed by the historical overview of the film photonovel and a springboard to a more detailed analysis of its key dimensions.

Some of these constraints concern the limitations of available material and the obligation to remain faithful to the original in several regards (but not in all, as is immediately shown by the frequent, yet never absolute, divergences between "source" and "target"). First, a film-photonovel maker has to work with images that have already been shot—normally, existing film stills that are fragments of the movie as shown in theaters. In some cases, set photographs and publicity pictures were also incorporated.[25] According to certain specialized fan sites (Ghera 2006), the set-pictures formula was even more constraining than the film-stills model, mainly because of the smaller number of pictures available (after all, modern films project twenty-four images per second, and the average length of a feature is around one hundred minutes). The close reading of some examples later in the book suggest, however, that this argument has its pitfalls.

In addition, the contracts between film companies and film-photonovel editors did not allow for individual or personal interpretation of the material. One was supposed to deliver a film in print that could function as a double of the movie, purchased by an audience eager to relive the filmic experience or to possess a substitute for a film that they had missed. Obviously, this commercial ethic of faithfulness did not mean that film photonovels were always close to the meaning and form of the adapted movie. It does explain, however, why the genre did not aspire to creatively rework its material. Our knowledge of these contacts and contracts is limited, yet the overall reading of any film photonovel never discloses any real attempt to adapt the filmic images or the plot of the movies freely, which attests to the power of the implicit or explicit rule of "faithfulness." Film photonovels do change the movies that they adapt, but they always reuse the visual material of the film and do not manipulate the basic structure of the work.

Even more important is a third category of constraints, namely, those that come from the adoption of the photonovel format. For contemporary readers, the film-photonovel policy of closely following the rules of this lowbrow format may seem astonishing, but in the ruthlessly competitive magazine market of the postwar years, this decision was logical. Film-photonovel producers, that is, publishers, simply wanted to cash in on the success of the dominant magazine formula—and that was the photonovel. The film photonovel inherited five main constraints from the photonovel, and they were present and active in all types of film photonovels.

To start with, it is necessary to highlight the reuse of the basic layout of the photonovel formula. As described above, the sequential arrangement of photographs on a page can take numerous forms, but the photonovel almost organically adhered to a page composition based on the three-tier model, each tier having, in principle, two (a maximum of three) images of slightly varied width. This format became the default option for most photonovel makers, and was almost immediately adopted by the film-photonovel industry as well. This kind of constraint may seem simple and logical, but it had tremendous consequences for at least two decisive aspects of visual storytelling, since in many cases it forced the recropping of the images. In film-photonovel versions of a movie, the aspect ratio, that is the relationship of the width of the image to its height, was often modified in order to adjust the film stills or set pictures to what readers used to the photonovel language expected. Moreover, and this was absolutely crucial, the necessity of offering a simultaneous view of some images—something G. E. Lessing would call images "next to another" (*nebeneinander*) instead of images "one after the other" (*nacheinander*) (Lessing [1766] 1984)—brutally disrupted the basic economy of linear, sequential storytelling.

A second constraint refers to the combination of words and images on the page. Here the theoretical possibilities were very diverse, but the photonovel discovered by trial and error a set of standards that were rapidly adopted by the industry, such as the inclusion of text in the image (more or less as in comics); the superposition of handwritten text on the picture's surface (which remained visible under the words); the encoding of the difference between sentence case and all uppercase lettering (the former referring to the characters' speech; the latter, to the narrator's voice); and, in contrast with most types of comics, the presence of words in designated areas of the image (ideally, at the top of the image). The most vital constraint concerned the necessary presence of the image: photonovels have the reputation of being loquacious, not because they use many words but because there are few panels without words. This constraint was naturalized. It goes without saying that there was absolutely nothing self-evident about it.

A third constraint was dictated by the publishing format and context of the photonovel, which were those of women's magazines, with their usual size (in the late 1940s, slightly larger than a sheet of A4 paper), volume (approximately forty to sixty pages per issue), periodicity (for example, weekly rather than monthly), and above all, content policy (based on the combination of visual fiction storytelling with a small number of highly ritualized additional sections, such as letters to the editor, the horoscope, a movie gossip column, and an article on fashion or housekeeping). Film photonovels adopted this model yet diverged from it in several key aspects. Although severely streamlined by the house rules of the series in which they appeared, they were presented as complete stories, whereas the photonovel magazines generally combined installments of several serialized stories that ran simultaneously. Film-photonovel magazines also tended to have more pages than photonovel magazines, a way of elevating an otherwise lowbrow production.

A fourth constraint, subtle yet crucial, involved the images themselves, which were selected or modified to adhere to the types of images that worked well in a photonovel. The implicit norm for a camera shot was situated between the medium shot and the close-up. The norm for content matter obeyed the aesthetics of the portrait rather than the action picture, often completely neglecting the background (the frequent denunciation of photonovel images as stiff and artificially posed is a crude misreading of what the genre imposed). The implications of these constraints are evident. But as with all authentic constraints, it is possible to understand them as an opportunity instead of a restraint.

Last, the horizon of the photonovel imposed a dominant thematic and narrative mode: that of the melodrama, which encompasses ideas of persecuted innocence, mistaken identities, and love as sacrifice (Brooks [1976] 1995) and involves a wide range of strongly visualized rhetorical devices underlining the dimension of the struggle between good and evil in the private and domestic sphere of love. Melodrama cannot be reduced to a stereotypical combination of happy endings, romance, and kitsch, although the contrary is often asserted in studies critical of these forms of lowbrow entertainment for women. Adherence to the tenets of modernism did build a horizon of expectations that influenced how movies were turned into film photonovels, an operation that systematically increased the over-sentimental and aggrandized aspects of the original material.

Each of these constraints—none of which could be put aside during the adaptation process—raises numerous questions. The most general and important of these result from the so-called semiotic gap, which refers to the material differences between the adapted and the adapting sign systems, as well as to the unusually narrow status and interpretation of the fidelity issue.

A film photonovel could not transfer all aspects or elements of a movie to the new medium. To give some simple examples, the adaptation inevitably lost the film's soundtrack and the moving character of the projected images; it shifted from theatrical projection in a darkened theater to a mode of material to be read in a women's magazine that generally contained a broad range of other sections. Furthermore, it abandoned the logic of sequential storytelling in favor of a type of visual communication partly based on the juxtaposition of images on single or double spreads; it reduced the average length of the experience from ninety minutes (the running time of an average feature film) to the time needed to read roughly fifty pages of a film photonovel; it went from wide screen to small panels; and it "spoiled" the visual integrity of the pictures by adding an unrefined set of words (cinephile *doxa* in this period was still reluctant to subtitle, preferring poorly dubbed versions of foreign works to versions with well-translated subtitles; see Egoyan and Balfour 2004), to name but some of the most important distinctions between film and film photonovel.

On the other hand, the film photonovel was condemned to a superlative degree of fidelity. Unlike film adaptations of literary material, in which screenwriters and directors often change whatever they feel is necessary in order to produce a good movie, the film photonovel professionals suffered inescapable impositions from both the original movie and the photonovel format. The former could not be modified ad lib, since the adaptation process was considered a translation (in the narrow sense of the word), not an adaptation (in the more liberal sense of the term). The photonovel format functioned as a commercial and aesthetic echo chamber that determined what a film photonovel had to look like, namely, a photonovel based on a movie.

Generally speaking, scholars of the film photonovel have stressed the countless crude flaws of the genre. With a certain mix of sadism, for the critiques are harsh, and masochism—after all, those who like to denigrate the film photonovel are also its readers, and sometimes its (hidden) fans and collectors—critics have unceasingly hammered on the same three nails. First, film photonovels are accused of oversimplifying the original movies: the story they tell is always a watered-down version of the original. Second, critics like to deplore the heavy-handedness of these adaptations, which destroy all subtlety and polyphony, replacing them with a shallow and overly explicit framing of the story and its characters. Third, film photonovels are said to radically transform and streamline the movies. When trans-mediating movies, film photonovels add something that is absent from many of the original films, specifically, a melodramatic layer. This change is accomplished, for instance, by inventing lines of dialogue that are nonexistent in the movie or by covering the whole story with a persistent voice-over that tells what the characters are thinking in order to influence the reader's perception.

All this sounds only too familiar. It uncannily recalls the (now forgotten) decades-long debates on the adaptation of books into films, a real mission impossible (unless the books were bad—that is, could not have been spoiled by the naturally degrading move from word to image). This is the irony of history: film is no longer the villain but the victim. Yet if we want to take seriously the idea that adaptations are independent works, whether they are works of art or not, we should start looking at film photonovels in a different light: not as problems or failures but as problem-solving machines. It is from this perspective that I analyze the poetics of a forgotten medium that deserves a second look.

Coda

The appendix to this book offers a detailed survey of the magazines, in Italian and in French, that published film photonovels during and after the golden age. To have a better understanding of the analyses to come, it may be helpful to chart the most important ones and to sketch their relative positions in the field. For although film photonovels occupied a particular niche of lowbrow cultural production, status was not unimportant. All film-photonovel magazines were equal, but some were more equal than others. In fact, the notion of the magazine cannot be separated from that of the publisher: publishers were definitely unequal, and some of them had series with better reputations than others. According to the formal criteria (among others) discussed above, the upper-level publishers in Italy were Bozzesi and La Lanterna Magica. The latter was also the first film-photonovel publisher active in France, predating Les Éditions mondiales / Cino Del Duca and Mon Film (the publisher of the magazine with the same name). Each publisher managed one or more flagship series, such as *Star Ciné Roman* (Bozzesi), *Nous Deux Film* (Les Éditions mondiales), and *Mon Film* (Mon Film). Other publishers had an intermediary position, the most commercially dynamic being Ponzoni in Italy as well as in France, and Artima in France (bought by Les Presses de la Cité in 1962). Others had poor reputations, and the selection of examples included in the following chapters do justice to all three categories: upper level, intermediary, and low.

3 / Word and Image, Telling and Showing

A bimedial medium, the film photonovel combines words and images to convey a story. It is not enough, however, to merely study the interaction between word and image on the page if the goal is to achieve a complete view of how the story is told. A more general category is needed; that is, one that encompasses the opposition between telling and showing (Gaudreault 2009). The analysis of telling and showing mechanisms is crucial for understanding how a certain type of communication with the reader or viewer is established. To formulate the basis for this category, we turn our attention to the relative presence or absence of a narrative voice in the production of the plot, distinguishing between showing and telling narrative modes. In the showing mode, the reader or the viewer has the (false) impression that the story is telling itself, while in the telling mode, the narrator's voice is directly experienced. Showing is a technique that seems to put more weight on a reader's or viewer's interpretation; in contrast, telling is often seen as a mode that leads to an interpretation of the text or the image in the way intended by the narrator (and behind this narrator there are also, at least for many readers and viewers, the implied narrator and the real author, but that is another discussion).

In practice, these differences are rarely clear-cut, but that does not diminish the hermeneutical value of establishing the telling-versus-showing distinction. I use this overall framework to investigate the relationships between words and images in the film photonovel and briefly analyze some characteristic examples.

House-Style Narrators

The basic question is very simple and therefore tricky: who tells the story in the film photonovel? At first sight, trying to answer such a question looks futile. Narratological analyses of bimedial narratives often distinguish between verbal and visual narrators (Verstraeten 2009), specifying that it is necessary to incorporate the active presence of a so-called meganarrator in these two voices (Gaudreault 2009). In this line of analysis, the focus is on who is in charge of dispatching and controlling what can be seen (images) and what can be read or heard (text).

For the film photonovel, the question of narration is more complex. Film photonovels are adaptations whose readers were aware of this adaptive status (in some cases, the audience had a direct and active knowledge of the original). For that reason, the telling-versus-showing distinction was often manipulated as it was transferred to the new genre. Further, the film photonovel appeared in a specific editorial and publishing context, that of a periodical, which reconfigured the notion of voice in new forms. The film photonovel was less an independent work than part of a magazine issue containing a variety of contributions and multiple voices.

In short, the tension between telling and showing is part of a larger whole: before and perhaps after reading a film photonovel, a consumer might view the movie, which includes the visual culture surrounding the film as well as the hype that it produces. This diversity was not a mere mosaic of voices, for each periodical was defined by its own "editorial voice" (Souchier 2007), which was the magazine equivalent of the meganarrator of a bimedial work. This editorial voice did not necessarily belong to a living person; it both emanated from and produced the symphony of contributions and voices found between the covers of the magazine. These tendencies can be understood as the house style of the magazine if the notion of house style is not reduced to just typographical matters, which are nonetheless important. House style generally concerns the selection and arrangement of the different sections that constitute the sequence of a magazine (a simple example: the relationship between reader and magazine is influenced by the presence or absence of a "letters to the editor" section); the style and tone of each section (in some cases, the letters to the editor section does not contain real letters but messages made up by an editor as a simple trick to "naturalize" the ideologically loaded answers provided by the magazine; see Cardone 2004a); the visual design, the look and feel of the magazine (which is roughly the same for film photonovels, with some slight differences: answers to letters to the editor, for example, can be signed by a pseudonym, a so-called expert or pundit, or even a movie star). Although one never knows "who is who" in these types of publications, the editorial voice is undoubtedly there and immediately recognizable to the audience. The editorial voice steers the reception of the magazine to a certain extent, and the audience accepts or refuses this guidance by either continuing to buy the magazine or dropping it. Since subscriptions in this market segment were infrequent, the strong editorial voice was unmistakably a marketing substitute for the absence of serialization.

Yet editorial voice and house style represent more than a network of voices that determine a certain type of reading. They also had a direct impact on how the film photonovel adapted movies. In this regard, it is crucial to take a closer look at the work's peritext (Genette [1987] 1997)—that is, the thresholds that introduce the work to the reader and serve as a lock or partition between the "world" and the "work." The peritext is not just an embellishment, although its aesthetic function is vital. It has several other functions, which are sometimes inseparable from the visual pleasure it provides. The most important functions of the peritext can be summarized as follows: the classification and identification of the textual object; the presentation and summary of the contents; the promotion of the work as a commercial object; and guidance on how to use the text. This list is far from exhaustive, and these functions of course overlapped and reinforced one another. For the film photonovel, which was always part of a magazine, the efficacy of the peritext was essential, as can be concluded from its relative quantity. It can often be difficult to distinguish text from peritext, for if the "text" of a film photonovel magazine is taken to be the pages occupied by the film photonovel itself, the textual or peritextual status of many of the other pages is not always easy to determine. The question, then, is how to interpret the letters to the editor section, the horoscope of the week, advertisements, the pinup centerfold, the short photonovel (used as a page filler when the film photonovel was not long enough to occupy the whole issue), and so forth. At first sight, none of these elements has a direct relationship with the content of the film photonovel (the centerfold pinup, for instance, does not necessarily relate to the adapted movie, and the advertisements may concern items or services that have nothing to do with the theme of the film photonovel). Yet they all "contaminate" or at least strongly influence the reading of the film photonovel.

Actually, the film photonovel goes much further in the integration of text and peritext than traditional publications in book format. Here, the strength of the peritext is such that the classic hierarchy of both levels—Genette is adamant in stressing the necessity to distinguish between what really matters, the text, and what is no more than an accompanying element, the peritext—is subject to change. Moreover, the film photonovel's peritext is twofold, namely, that of the magazine and that of the film photonovel itself. Each of these two dimensions is divided into at least two levels. The magazine's peritext is both general and singular: it concerns the magazine as a whole as well as the sections found next to the film photonovel, all of them with their own peritexts. The film photonovel's peritext is also a two-step mechanism, for one reads first the peritextual translation of the film credits and only after that the proper peritext of the film photonovel adaptation. But between all these levels and elements there is a strong continuity, which can be related to the notion of "flow" as theorized by Raymond Williams ([1970] 1974) in his study of commercial television and its consciously produced overlap of program types, such as information and entertainment.

Peritext Level 1: How the Magazine Frames the Film Photonovel

Each of the magazine's peritextual elements, unified by the overarching editorial voice or house style, contributes to a global form that builds a horizon of expectations for the intended readership. In this peritextual framework, some elements are systematically placed in the foreground. First, and perhaps stereotypically, the magazine's peritext produces a methodical emphasis on the melodramatic aspects of life, both in a positive and a negative light. The information on the movie stars and other celebrities (directors, authors, scriptwriters, showbiz performers, stage performers) is presented through rose-colored glasses; the rich and famous are invariably happy and enviable. In the other sections—short stories, serialized novels, complementary photonovels—however, this image is more nuanced. This more nuanced perspective provides insight into the dark side of passionate love and the unavoidable flip side of lives torn between heaven and hell. In short, the magazine's peritext blends the melodramatic imagination with the aggrandizement and overstatement of the central element in the magazine, the film photonovel.

Second, the leading role in a film photonovel is held by the actor and not by the director. This is not unusual in film culture. In spite of the rise of the auteur cult in the movie industry during that period, as seen in the way that the name of the director is acknowledged in some film-photonovel peritexts (see below), the bottom line of the magazine's peritext is crystal clear: a film is made by the star (singular or plural, with strict divisions among gender roles). All front and back covers show movie stars. Nearly all complementary texts, pictures, and reports concern the actors, rarely the directors. A good example here is "Finestra sul Cortile," the Italian film photonovel version of Hitchcock's *Rear Window* (1954), published in 1955 in the prestigious *Cineromanzo Gigante* series of La Lanterna Magica.[1] Despite being published in a prestigious series and giving the director's name in the film photonovel's credits (in "cheaper" publications, this was far from the rule), the work's initial peritext on the inside cover is exclusively focused on the lead actor, Jimmy Stewart, as if Alfred Hitchcock was nothing more than an exchangeable employee of Paramount Studios. This seemed to be the way he was seen in the popular press before the French awarded him auteur status par excellence (Truffaut [1966] 1985). Bizarrely enough, the other missing name is Grace Kelly's, equally absent from the initial and the final peritext (the last pages of the magazine are devoted to other movies' celebrities and reportages). Generally speaking, the importance given to the movie star in the film-photonovel magazines is a supplementary factor that strengthens the cohesion of the periodical. Whatever the material inside the publication, it all orbits the star.

The third key aspect of the magazine's peritext is the flip side of the celebration of the movie star: how film-photonovel periodicals bridged the gap between the glamour of the film business and the dismal dreariness of daily life for most readers. For the film photonovel, more was involved than daydreaming or escapism. The direct link between the newer film photonovel and the older photonovel obliged the former to repeat what the latter had already managed to achieve successfully, namely, the opportunity to leave behind one's own life and become a real star. In the beginning, photonovels were famous for their castings: all readers, female or male, were invited to send in their pictures or to come to regularly organized casting calls held next to the photo studios or on locations where photonovels were shot. The lucky winners were offered the chance to play a role in a photonovel, with the hope that they would be selected for a role in the real film industry. Everybody knew that some of the most famous Italian stars of the 1950s had started their careers in the photonovel business, the usual breeding ground for stars and starlets. The film photonovel could not, of course, make such an offer, but attempts were made to "help" the reader—male and female, contrary to the biases and prejudices that may exist in the eyes of most critics—surmount the abyss between real life and dream life.[2] Key to this policy were the advertisements, which were—not astonishingly—more abundant in cheaper magazines (buyers of more expensive and comparatively more upscale magazines did not have the same need to correct their self-images, and the larger print runs of those magazines made them less dependent on publicity revenues).

What are these advertisements about? They are about everything that seemed to be missing from the reader's life, all the while presenting celebrities' lives as the model. These advertisements could be purchased for next to nothing, and they included elements of physical enhancement (products for breast lifting for female readers, products to grow and become a "tall man" for male readers, snake oil substances for all kinds of smaller and bigger diseases) as well as elements of psychological well-being: specialized services for winning back a lover, finding the ideal match, marrying a millionaire (for the ladies), and enhancing sexual performance (for the gents)—or, more modestly, learning how to dance. The film photonovel was both a beauty parlor and a bureau for life advice that constructed a kind of embodied reception. The magazine made a medical and psychological profile, or rather a diagnosis, of its readership, one that was in stark contrast to the examples offered by the stars, but overtly comparable to the troubles depicted in the film photonovels and most peritextual sections. At the same time, the magazine offered anything needed to fix these flaws, with the solutions being advertised next to the film photonovels, and the results of these solutions were fictionally displayed inside the world of the film photonovel. Here the women appear to have the advertised breast structure (the changing fashions are easy to follow!). Here the men do not suffer from the problems hinted at elsewhere (their bodies are both slim and beefy, the men tender yet always ready to act). Finally, men and women in the film photonovels succeed in solving the problems of extreme passion and the misunderstandings such passion might provoke, never surrendering to the external constraints of society. The flow from peritextual advertisements to film-photonovel fictions and vice versa never discloses any real gap.

Peritext Level 2: How the Film Photonovel Frames Its Own Story

Given the strength of the peritextual framing provided by the magazine, the peritext of the film photonovel cannot be analyzed as an autonomous level of the work—that is, solely in relation to the film photonovel that it is intended to complement. It would be a mistake to suggest that the main features of the magazine's context are all mechanically reproduced in this second layer, but the triple focus on melodrama, celebrity culture, and relevance of the fictional world for the reader's daily life is not something that can be disregarded when one enters the film photonovel. Even if the need for a willing suspension of disbelief cannot be denied, the triple awareness of genre constraints, the presence of the work's heroes and heroines in real life, and the possibility of getting closer to another world offers a permanent echo chamber for what the reader will uncover in the work.

The proper peritext of the film photonovel must always be linked with this general framework, hence the swiftness with which the film photonovel performs the melodramatic reframing of the movie's content. Although melodrama is key to the genre, the reframing of the story is easily attainable, since the whole context of the magazine has prepared the reader for this conversion. In addition, this turn to melodrama distracts from any excessive emphasis on the movie stars in the credit panels of the film photonovel: a tactical move that can be explained by the difficulty of linking the content with the reader's daily life. The world of the stars is treated in the magazine's peritext, so in the film photonovel peritext there is little need to further accentuate this implicit dialogue with the readers, who imagine themselves in the lives of the rich and famous.

The proper peritext of the film-photonovel fiction generally entails two parts, which it is important to disentangle, for their form, content, and scope are distinct (fig. 3.1). First, the opening frame of any film photonovel offers a panel in diptych form, generally over the full width of the printed page, which merges and transforms two aspects of the adapted movie. The summary-mode sketches—that is, the outline form that a film poster or an illustration would take—depict the principal theme of the movie: it contains an image that "summarizes" the whole film while further highlighting the key place of the stars. It shows what the film is about at a glance, often the age-old battle for love. The "celebrity" mode continues the ongoing focus on the star. Moreover, this "title frame" gathers those elements of the film credits that help identify the source material of the adaptation. In general, the more serious and prestigious a film photonovel tries to be, the more information that these credits include. In some cases, the opening frame has no credits at all, which tends to make the identification of the adapted film almost impossible, except for specialists of certain categories of B movies. In most cases however, the names of the actors and, to a lesser extent, that of the director and the production company are mentioned, always within the same panel. Certain magazines—the impact of the house style is very clear here—split these two aspects. They give the title in the opening frame and relocate all the other credits to the bottom of the page, outside the pictures' surfaces. A typical example here would be *Ciné-Révélation*, a magazine that occupied an intermediary

FIGURE 3.1. *"L'Adorable Voisine" (*Bell, Book and Candle, *1958, Richard Quine),* Les Films pour vous, *7 January 1961, p. 3.*

position between the film photonovel and the less prominent photonovel, which rarely supplied this supplementary credit information during the period. In short, the filmic original is generally present, yet dramatically transformed.

Second—and here the dominant mode shifts from transformation, with numerous deletions and erasures, to addition—the film photonovel creates a contact zone between the technical peritext of the opening frame and the descriptive peritext that immediately follows. The material form (size and position) of this second peritextual zone may vary widely among magazines, each following its house style, but the basic content remains unaltered. The idea is to help the reader enter the story world while maintaining the melodramatic character of the narrative about to unfold.

Let us examine two representative examples of this general law of the genre. Their overly explicit character does not require much discussion. The first is from the *Rebel Without a Cause* adaptation. In the voice-over that opens as well as ends the story, the overarching impact of this narrative intervention is evident:

> Minuit a depuis longtemps sonné dans une ville de province d'un État quelconque d'Amérique. Ce qu'il y arrive pourrait arriver partout. À dix ans de la guerre, dans la grande république, une fermentation secrète agite l'agglomération humaine. Grands et petits conflits, drames, tragédies, inquiétudes où fleurissent aussi de soudaines et étranges rédemptions. Comme toujours depuis des millions d'années, l'humanité creuse avec peine sa route dans le roc compact de son destin. Comme toujours encore, les patrouilles d'avant-garde, les victimes, les pionniers et les vaincus, ce sont les jeunes, les tous [*sic*] jeunes, ceux qui traversent la saison de l'adolescence douloureuse et heureuse à la fois. Le jour de Pâques vient de finir et, conséquence habituelle des jours de fête, les postes de police sont en pleine activité.
>
> La voix de Judy s'arrête dans un soupir puis tout retombe dans le silence qui les entoure avec la vaste nuit. Sous la voûte du ciel, les hommes tissent infatigablement leur destin et le ciel est noir, les étoiles lointaines et indifférentes. Cependant l'heure la plus sombre est celle qui précède l'aube et, à l'horizon apparaîtra sous peu le premier frisson de lumière! Et c'est ainsi qu'un pâle sourire pointe sur les lèvres de Judy. La main de Jim l'effleure comme une caresse légère, religieusement, comme on touche une fleur. Jamais ils n'oublieront cet instant, l'aube d'une vie nouvelle! FIN.

> [The midnight bell has tolled for quite some time now in some rural American town. What happens there could happen anywhere. Ten years after the war, in the great republic, a secret fermentation shakes the human agglomeration: conflicts great and small, tragedies, misfortunes, and anxieties, where sudden and strange redemptions also flourish. As always, for millions of years, humankind is painfully carving its way through the dense rock of its destiny. And also as always, the front-line patrols, the victims, the pioneers, and the defeated are the young ones, the very young ones, those who pass through the season of adolescence at once painful and happy. Easter is just over, and as usually happens at holidays, the police stations are extremely busy.
>
> Judy's voice ends in a whisper, and then everything returns to the silence that surrounds them in the infinite night. Under the dome of the sky, men tirelessly weave their destiny, and the sky is black, the stars are faraway and indifferent. Yet the darkest hour is the one before dawn, and soon the first shiver of the light will appear on the horizon. And so a pale smile will appear on Judy's lips. Jim's hand lightly touches her in a soft caress, religiously, as if touching a flower. Never will they forget this moment, the beginning of a new life! THE END.]

The second example, a prestigious international all-star film adaptation of a European existentialist novel, Marguerite Duras's *Un Barrage contre le Pacifique* (1950, translated as *The Sea Wall* in 1952; the title of the 1958 René Clément movie is *This Angry Age*), is all the more interesting since it was adapted twice, first as a short-story film photonovel (five pages, in *Ciné-Révélation*, Editor, 1958) and then in a more conventionally sized version (sixty-three pages, *Ciné-Succès*, Mercurio, 1959). This pattern was repeated in the *Rebel Without a Cause* adaptation made by a different publisher. In both cases, the typical middlebrow romance style serves as the universalizing and melodramatizing mechanism informing the rewrites. The short-story version has an opening text panel and a conclusive narrative voice-over, which read as follows:

> Ceci se passait au cours des dernières années de paix dont a joui l'Extrême-Orient, quelque part dans une zône [*sic*] côtière de l'Indochine française. C'est l'histoire mille fois répétée, mais inconnue, de l'acharnement de quelques uns à faire d'un désert marécageux, une terre aux riches récoltes, celle aussi de beaucoup dont l'existence ne fut que le déroulement de multiples incidents, qui bouleversaient leurs projets, les anéantissaient ou, parfois, mais rarement, permettaient leur épanouissement.

Autour d'eux, les villageois, pleins d'entrain, travaillaient sans arrêt pour reconstruire la digue. . . . Une digue qui les mettrait désormais à l'abri de toute tempête. . . .

Et vint un jour où, les travaux étant très avancés, Michaël décida de quitter le domaine . . . Suzanne et Joseph l'accompagnèrent jusqu'à l'autobus.

Michaël jeta un regard interrogateur à Suzanne. . . . Un peu pâle, la jeune fille s'écarta de son frère et, brusquement, rejoignit Forestier. . . . Au même instant, le vieil autobus s'ébranla.

[This happened during the final years of peace that the Far East has enjoyed, somewhere in a place along the coast of French Indochina. It is the story, told a thousand times yet still unknown, of the hard work of those trying to make a swampy desert into a land of rich harvests; the story of many of those whose life was nothing but the unfolding of countless incidents that shattered and destroyed their projects but that sometimes, though very seldom, allowed these projects to flourish.

Around them, the high-spirited villagers worked incessantly to rebuild the dyke. . . . A dyke that would shelter them from any tempest. . . .

And then came the day when, the work being almost finished, Michael decided to leave the domain . . . Suzanne and Joseph accompanied him to the bus.

Michael looked at Suzanne inquiringly. . . . Slightly pale, the young girl moved away from her brother and went back to Forester. . . . At that very moment, the old bus set off.

And this is the opening and closing narrative voice-over of the longer version of the same work:

La passionnante histoire que nous allons vous raconter se déroule dans une atmosphère amère et brûlante où, à chaque instant la vie risque de se transformer en drame et l'amour en passion. La famille Dufresne, composée de la mère et de ses deux enfants, Joseph et Suzanne, vit en Extrême-Orient, sur une côte du pacifique où de vastes rizières côtoient leur implacable ennemie: la mer. (p. 3)

L'autocar se met en marche. . . . Il s'éloigne lentement. . . . Oui, c'est vrai: chacun a son destin déjà tracé. Mais Suzanne a le cœur gros, en se préparant à affronter le sien.

Pourtant, c'est un avenir d'amour et sans doute de bonheur qui l'attend. . . . Mais une partie d'elle-même reste là-bas, avec son frère, à l'abri de cette digue de ciment dont leur pauvre mère rêva jusqu'à son dernier souffle. . . .

Son regard n'arrive pas à se détacher de cette vaste surface d'eau? saumâtre. . . . Il ne se laisse pas de caresser la silhouette chérie de son frère. Et plus cette silhouette se rapetisse. . . . plus elle grandit dans le cœur de Suzanne! FIN.

[The passionate story that we are about to tell you takes place in a bitter and burning atmosphere where life can, at any time, become tragedy and love become passion. The Dufresne family, a mother and her two children, Joseph and Suzanne, lives in the Far East, on a Pacific coast where vast rice fields can be found next to what is their merciless enemy: the sea.

The bus leaves. . . . It moves off slowly. . . . Yes, it is true: for all of us, our destiny has already been set. Yet Suzanne's heart is heavy as she prepares to confront her own.

However, it is a future full of love and, no doubt, happiness that awaits her. . . . But a part of her stays there, with her brother, behind the sheltering concrete dyke that their poor mother dreamed of until her last breath. . . .

She cannot take her eyes away from the vast surface of brackish water. . . . Her eyes can't stop caressing the beloved silhouette of her brother. And then this silhouette becomes smaller . . . the more it grows in Suzanne's heart! THE END.]

In comparison with the adaptations of *Rebel Without a Cause* and *This Angry Age*—two movies that are anything but melodramas, even though they tended to assume these characteristics in film-photonovel treatments—the narrative accompaniment of real melodramas is allowed to remain dramatically sober. These works do not need this type of reframing, hence the very simple, even rather dry introduction and conclusion in this kind of film photonovel. A good example here is the mother of all modern Italian melodramas, Raffaello Matarazzo's *Catene* (1949), which opens and closes in this way:

L'histoire que nous allons vous raconter est une histoire profondément humaine qui retracera l'amour et la douleur qui s'abattent sur une femme touchée injustement dans ses affections.

> Les bras grands ouverts de la petite fille sont pour eux la plus belle des promesses. Une vie nouvelle qui s'ouvre devant eux.
>
> [The story we are going to tell is a profoundly human story that will bring back the love and pain that befall a woman unfairly hurt in her affections.
>
> The wide-open arms of the little girl are, for them, the most beautiful of promises. A new life starts for them.]

What is fascinating in these narrative panels is the ambivalence of their status, which prompts a question: do they still belong to the domain of the peritext? If so, they would have a function similar to that of the presentation text generally found on the back cover of the film photonovel. Or are they already part of the fictional universe of the film photonovel? The first appearance of the voice-over guides the reader through the whole story. Narratively, viewing these panels as part of the fictional universe of the film photonovel is certainly accurate. One of the most striking features of the film photonovel is the creation of a narrator's voice that systematically "tells" what is "shown" by the images. But it is plausible to assert that the opening frame and the narrative clarification it offers cannot be separated from the peritextual domain. Indeed, the narrator's voice, which accompanies the reader throughout the rest of the story, is doing what the readers expect from a peritext: it classifies the work (identifies the genre); it gives a summary of the content (succeeds in defining in one panel who, where, what, when, and why); it stresses the importance of the story (could work as a blurb); it provides the reader with an interpretative frame (addresses issues of good and evil, faith and forgiveness, betrayal and tolerance, and so forth from the start); and it functions as a transition between context and text (highlights the importance of the lack of images, which take all the available space immediately after the opening text panel). The "telling" dimension overpowers the "showing" dimension, less in quantitative than in qualitative terms. The initial peritext may be short, but its place is absolutely strategic, and it sets the tone for the rest of the work. The same mechanism is seen at the end of the story. The narrative voice that manifests at the beginning of the film photonovel punctuates the whole work with complementary information, which persists in the final panel of the work, where it explicitly underlines, in ultradidactic ways, the moral undertone of the narrative. A final caption or text panel always specifies the lesson to be drawn from the story. The higher or deeper meaning that this final panel highlights is not that of the movie but that of the story as it is reframed as a film-photonovel melodrama.

This blurring of the boundaries between text and peritext—more precisely, the combination of textual and peritextual functions in the opening and closing frames—strengthens the multiple exchanges between the huge number of diverse and yet strangely converging elements contained in a film photonovel.

Given the importance of this opening frame, which is a fundamental building block of the film photonovel, two other remarks are necessary: one on the form and content of the corresponding closing panel and one on the specific quality of the narrative voice, which can be determined by following two paths. Indeed, although most opening panels are simply added to the original material, the narrative voice "overwrites" the filmic voice-over.

In all cases, the narrative voice remains consistent, endlessly repeating the morally conservative and ideologically normalized message. This stance is often at odds with the subtlety of the work being adapted, but not with the overall production of the magazines, which offer a well-balanced mix of pure entertainment and moralizing intermezzi. In this way, the narrative voice functions as a genre marker, and its excessively intrusive tone at the beginning and end of each film photonovel must not have gone unnoticed by its readers. The concluding remarks of the film photonovel serve two purposes. Besides echoing the opening statement of the voice-over, they bridge the gap between the film-photonovel fiction and the rest of the magazine's often lengthy peritext that follows, whose role and place differ from those of the peritext in other publications. In the film photonovel, the peritext is both the initial threshold to the fiction (read before entering the fictional world) and the final threshold (read after leaving that same fictional world). These concluding thresholds appear, of course, in other publications, but in the film photonovel they are sometimes as large as the work itself.

A second type of narrative intervention is more than an addition and, in some respects, a deletion. Some films already have voice-overs of their own, and it would have been relatively easy to reuse them to perform the peritextual functions of the added voice-over. Yet this was not what happened, as can be seen in the 1961 Bozzesi adaptation of *The Apartment* (Billy Wilder, 1960). In this film, the credits and opening scenes are presented in a spectacular voice-over by Jack Lemmon, who plays a modern schlemiel involved in a charming love story that is fundamental to the plot of the film. First-run audiences must have been (pleasantly) surprised by Jack Lemmon's rapid speech, probably the fastest voice-over in film history. In the film photonovel, this voice-over is replaced by a third-person narrator who, almost thriftily, delivers a small part of the information initially provided by Lemmon.[3] It takes Lemmon thirty-eight seconds to perform this part of his speech, which we hear as a voice-over during the projection of a classic zoom from the panoramic view of the city to the hands of the clerk. The key moments of the visual sequence are neatly reproduced in the first page of the film photonovel adaptation.[4] Lemmon's matter-of-fact speech appears as follows in print:

> A city has two different faces. It can be merry, exciting, and full of promise for those who live there and hope for a better life, or it can be as sad as a desolate desert for those who survive in the most piteous solitude. In that sense, New York is at the same time the merriest and the saddest place on earth. Millions of buildings, billions of business dollars, and, on top of that, progress, automation, industrial civilization. There is no place where a heart can feel lonelier than in this Tower of Babel.
>
> Calvin Baxter, a young man whose friends call him Bud, is one of these lonely people. And the office he works in has nothing to satisfy his insatiable thirst for human understanding.
>
> He has a job at the Consolidated Life Insurance Company, one of the biggest in America. Together with 31,259 other employees, he has his desk in a fifty-story building, a real human anthill.
>
> For three years Bud has worked there from 8:50 a.m. till 5:20 p.m., with a thirty-minute lunch break that he takes at the office's automated restaurant. This is where he works, in the premium department, section W, table number 85.

The reader's experience might be different from that of the spectator: the shift from first-person to third-person narrative and the replacement of a fast speaking voice with a recital of the bare minimum of information is a great loss. Yet functionally, the result is the same in the film and on the page. A narrative voice that overwrites a filmic voice-over has the same intended effects as those pursued by the "invention" of a voice-over that is not present in the adapted movie. The fact that different structures—sometimes replacement, sometimes addition—aim at similar effects demonstrates the strength of the narrative function and the profile of the opening frame of the film photonovel. Whatever forms this panel may take, and whatever its origin may be, the final result never changes. The objective is always to fix the reader's interpretation before he or she starts reading.

The methodical foregrounding of the voice-over is an aspect of a more general issue related to the quasi impossibility of a pure showing in the film photonovel. The reasons for this difficulty are threefold. First, all popular genres tend to provide the most detailed information possible in order to avoid any disruption of the reader's fluid and rapid narrative comprehension. The text has to be as explicit as possible—a universal characteristic of popular writing. Second, even when the source material of the adaptation is a not a bimedial work, since it is perfectly possible to convert silent movies into film photonovels, the impact of the twin model of the photonovel and the film novel, two extremely talkative genres, is so overwhelming that the film photonovel cannot break this constraint and thus must always include the verbal equivalent of dialogue and voice-over narration. Finally, the available material, that is, a set of pictures, is not produced as the vehicle of an autonomous visual story; pictures can tell stories when arranged in sequences, but then the pictures should preferably be made according to a narrative program. This is not the case here, since the pictures of a film photonovel are taken from another work, always organized in direct interaction with a soundtrack that is no longer there and that the film photonovel has to restore or, more precisely, to reinvent.

Words and Images in Panels and Pages

Once a film photonovel starts, new questions emerge regarding how the characters' speech and the narrator's voice and agency are materialized on the page. One of the many criticisms of the film photonovel concerns its poor quality as well as the excessive use of verbal fragments, most panels being littered with captions and dialogues as silly as they are difficult to read. The examples shown in figures 3.2 through 3.4—the first one a variation on Dostoyevsky's *Crime and Punishment*, with a character hearing voices; the second one an effort displaying a lack of balance between texts and images; and the third one an amazing Spanish rewriting of Fellini's *The Nights of Cabiria*—"speak for themselves" in more than one sense. These selected (though somewhat typical) samples are ugly and even horrendous, whereas the true situation was of course more nuanced, as the analysis of a more balanced set of examples will demonstrate. Yet before discussing those works, it is necessary to briefly answer a few questions: What kind of text is found in film photonovels? How do these texts adapt spoken or written words in their reworkings of the film? How do texts and images interact on the page?

The first terms that need to be highlighted in this discussion are "reduction" and "simplification," which are not necessarily bad things,[5] despite impressions sometimes to the contrary. Instances of reduction are systemic. The narrative voice-over added to the filmic original usually

FIGURE 3.2. *"La Voix de la conscience"* (Crimen y castigo, *1951, Fernando de Fuentes),* Hebdo Roman, *20 July 1960, p. 11.*

FIGURE 3.3. *"Revoir Florence" (*Porta un bacione a Firenze*, 1955, Camillo Mastrocinque),* Roman Film*, 15 April 1958, p. 6.*

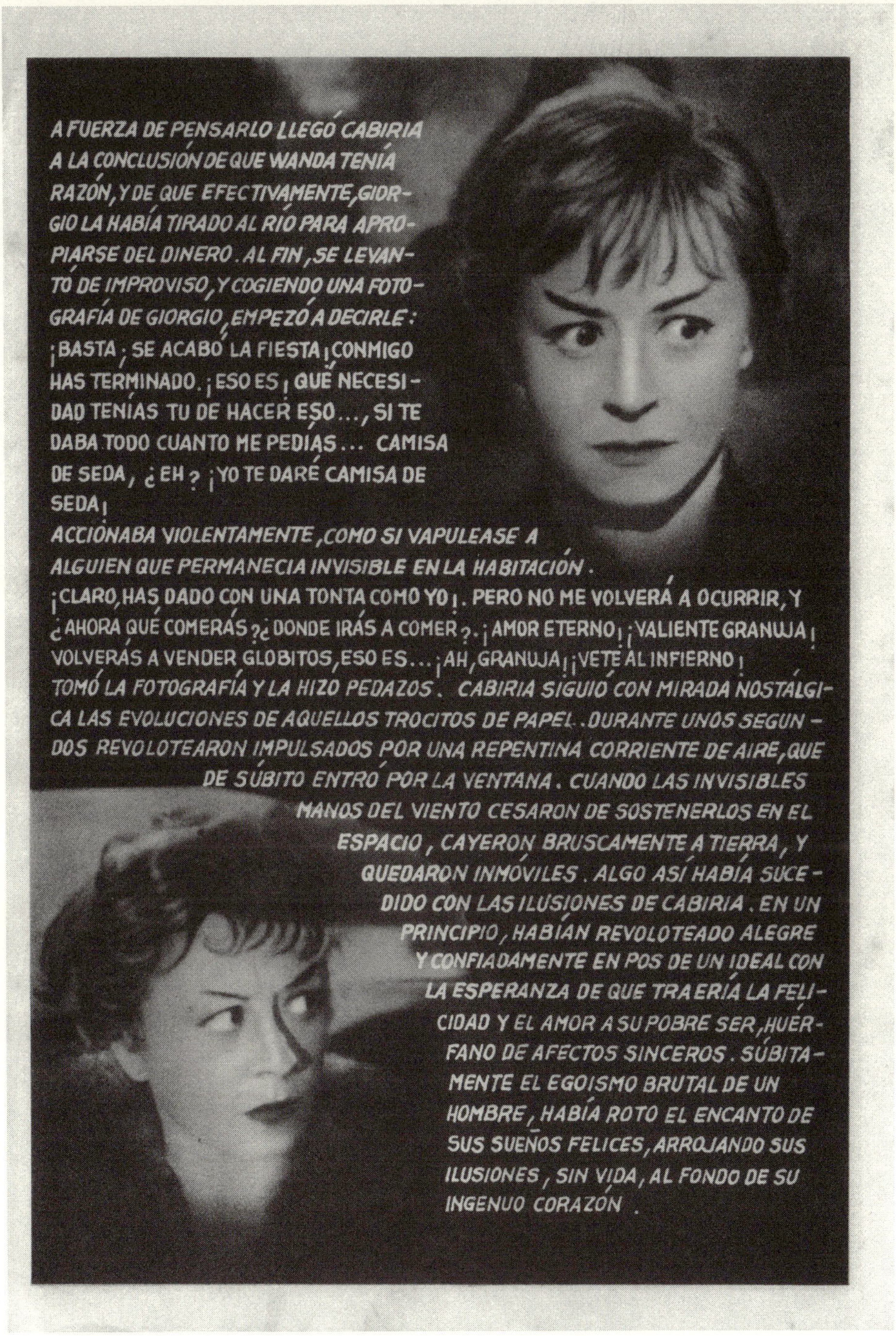

FIGURE 3.4. *"Las Noches de Cabiria"* (Le Notti di Cabiria, *1957, Federico Fellini),* Cine Ensueño, *1959, n.p. [10].*

simplifies and condenses the soundtrack. The loss of music and nonverbal aspects of the soundtrack is perhaps not radically different from what happens visually when color movies are remade into black-and-white film photonovels. The loss does not prevent the film photonovel from including numerous dance and ball scenes, despite the many problems these scenes may raise, given the static nature of the genre. More problematic is the loss of "suprasegmental" verbal information: when reproduced in print, voices lose their tone, rhythm, height, pitch, accent, and so on. In principle, it is possible to find some kind of visual compensation for this loss, but this is not what happens. The film photonovel normally refrains from using typographical enhancements to suggest speech differences. To put it more bluntly: on the page, characters scream and whisper in exactly the same way. An extreme example of such a flattening is the adaptation of Jacques Demy's 1964 *Les Parapluies de Cherbourg* (*The Umbrellas of Cherbourg*, starring Catherine Deneuve, here in her debut; the film score is by Michel Legrand). The film dialogue, even the most casual conversation, is sung as recitative, similar in style to an opera, but no allusion whatsoever is made to this quite exceptional feature in the film photonovel version, which likewise completely dismisses the delicate color work of the movie. The film photonovel not only drops the "suprasegmental" aspects of speech but also rewrites and banalizes the dialogue. Such a rewriting is practically inevitable when one tries to convert spoken language to written speech (published screenplays point out similar issues). The film photonovel, however, takes this rewriting to the extreme: first, by its simplification of the syntactic structure of many sentences (a typical example is the rewriting of an indirect construction into a direct one; instead of "I wonder what he is doing?" one normally finds, "What is he doing?"), and second, by its inveterate penchant for verbal clichés borrowed from the melodramatic tradition, as reflected, for instance, in the replacement of colloquial or vulgar terms with more bookish terms—there is no cursing in the film photonovel (for an analysis of the bowdlerizing Spanish translation of Fellini's 1957 *Le Notti di Cabiria*, see Cardone 2006).

Another key word is "streamlining." Readers minimally familiar with the codes of film photonovels know that they will find the same types of texts (narrative commentaries, character dialogue, and often words appearing in the photographed universe, such as letters or billboard signs) and that each type will be neatly separated from the others and adopt a different graphic style (the narrative voice-over will be in all-caps, and the speech or thought balloons will be in upper- and lowercase—or the former will be italicized and the latter not, or vice versa: it is the difference that matters). Each type will occupy a different space inside or outside the panels. Narrative comments may be inserted in separate text panels or in the upper or lower part of the image panel, whereas the speech or thought balloons always appear in the image panels, yet never in such a way that they can be confused with the narrative comments. When texts are directly added to the image, without special frames or background colors, the concern for a neat separation of types and levels remains. Everything is organized in such a way that readers can never mistake the narrative voice-over for the characters' speech or thoughts. In addition, the streamlining of the verbal dimension of the photonovel concerns issues of length and style. Most photonovels appear to have a consistent volume of comparable narrative comments and speech balloons. If they are rare and rather short in the beginning—or frequent and rather long—they will remain so until the end. As far as their stylistic register is concerned, surprisingly few film photonovels escape the linguistic stereotypes of the photonovel and the popular film novel, which copy the serialized nineteenth-century melodrama (see Sergio 2012 for a detailed reading of the linguistic particularities of this style as reflected in the photonovel). The slightly anachronistic language adheres to a kind of middle- to lowbrow idea of "good writing" that is no longer in use. Finally, it is crucial to stress that this general model is both universal and systematically customized. On the one hand, all film photonovels follow the same codes. As my analyses will show, the key principles of this formula were fixed by one of the leading publishers in Italy, Bozzesi, the inventor of the "classic" display of text and image in the film photonovel genre, in which elegance and simplicity reigned supreme. On the other hand, each magazine tried to customize the classic model in the hope that the difference would be noticeable without violating genre constraints.

A final key word is "simultaneity." This term, of course, should not be taken literally. In print, it is not possible to obtain a perfect temporal match between the single moment of a photograph and the longer or shorter span of time inextricably linked to a verbal utterance. Yet the film photonovel is characterized by a kind of meta-simultaneity, a combination of two mechanisms: first, the visual moment of the picture is always supposed to take place during the time of the verbal utterance, and second, the necessary copresence of text and image means that textless panels are almost forbidden (there are exceptionally few of them in the whole film-photonovel corpus, whereas most works contain several text panels without any images).[6] Additionally, the presence of excessively long verbal utterances or complexly structured dialogue is drastically reduced. We can turn to two famous examples to illustrate either case. In *Bitter Rice* (*Riso amaro*, Giuseppe De Santis, 1949), a landmark work of neorealist film, a long dance scene with Silvana Mangano contains only music and diegetic sound (hand clapping and singing), no dialogue. Given the crucial importance of this scene to the plot, it proved impossible to delete it in the adaptation, but in the film photonovel there is an interior monologue of the character dancing. This monologue, which is not present in the movie, helps the adaptation fit the word-and-image model of the film photonovel. *Bread, Love, and Jealousy* (*Pane, amore e gelosia*, Luigi Comencini, 1954) is the second part of the *Bread and Love* trilogy about Antonio Carotenuto, a middle-aged marshal of the carabinieri who tries to get married. The film signified the switch from original neorealism to "pink" neorealism (the trilogy is often seen as one of the first steps to commercially more viable, and more depoliticized, Italian comedy). In *Bread, Love, and Jealousy*, there are scenes of burlesque commedia dell'arte dialogue, which are fast and polyphonic with several persons speaking, shouting, gesticulating, and leaping at the same time. The film-photonovel adapter wisely chose to give a brief third-person summary of the story line and to illustrate such scenes with just one image.

In the telling-versus-showing debate, the visualization of the spoken word in the film photonovel represents the continued dominance of the telling mode. The text makes the meaning of the image more explicit, so much so that it is intrusive: not only because of the space that it occupies and the attention it draws to the verbal dimension of the work, but also because of its omnipresence. Adding a verbal commentary that underlines and paraphrases what can be seen without any problem in the image seems to be part of the film photonovel's DNA. Examples of the contrary style, namely, the dissociation of telling and showing in a panel, are very hard to find. As in all forms of popular fiction, the meganarrator tries to ensure that the reader understands everything without any effort, hence the sometimes bizarre but generically perfectly normal presence of explicative statements that say it all.

Suffice it to say that the text plays the leading role in a film photonovel. Text, not image, drives the story, and this hierarchy is apparent throughout the genre. The dominant position of the text may even jeopardize the role and the place of the image. In extreme cases, there is so much text that there is hardly any place left for the images, whose function becomes purely (and poorly) illustrative. Film photonovels are, however, much more than stories; they are also objects to look at, and, in this regard, the image comes back with a vengeance.

From Dawn till Sunset: The Rise and Fall of the "Classic Model"

The last section of this chapter proposes a comprehensive illustration of the interaction between word and image on the film photonovel's pages. I have selected four representative works, all in French, published by the four major publishers of the golden era (two Italian, two French), but in different periods (ranging from 1958 to 1966) and covering four genres. Mixing highbrow and lowbrow (an exotic adventure movie, a literary fairy tale, a Left Bank psychological drama, and a western), this selection aims to show the specific editorial policy of each magazine and the company behind it, as well as the transformations, whether small or substantial, of the film photonovel over time, from the so-called classic model to the progressive fading out of the genre.

In the beginning, the French film photonovel spoke Italian, at least in its visual language and design. Just before the Italian market for film photonovels suddenly collapsed, around 1957, several publishers adopted a new business model that relied on three closely related strategies: reducing or even abandoning the initially highly successful, but now rapidly waning, formula of adapting all kinds of major movies, either domestic or imported, into relatively luxurious magazine versions; shifting to cheaper formats and generally moving to lowbrow genre fiction; and exporting French translations of works published in Italian and, eventually, producing new film photonovels in French. From a material point of view, the Italian origin of several series and magazines is easy to detect, for example, via characteristic typos, such as "mistère" (Italian: *mistero*, French: *mystère*—the typical confusion between *i* and *y*). Italian origins are also visible in the survival of many Italian additions or supplements to the French translations. "Les Surprises du mariage" (*Roman d'amour*, 1961; Edisirio),[7] the French translation of an Italian original based on *We're Not Married!* (Edmund Goulding, 1952), tells a story whose plot is set in the heart of New England, although some topographical and other markers and inscriptions—"Italianized" in the first film photonovel version—were not replaced by their French equivalents, most likely due to a lack of time and attention. The first panel of the work gives a close-up of the name and address of a justice of the peace specializing in quick marriages: "MELVIN BUSH / GIUDICE DI PACE / LICENZA C/ MATRIMONIO $?"

In France, there were homegrown versions of the film photonovel, so the Italian publishers did not have to start from scratch. Through trial and error, many of the word-and-image problems raised by the first film photonovels had been resolved. Some of these problems had to do with the legibility of both elements. The ability to print words on pictures instead of next to them, for instance, while maintaining a good visual contrast between both without any overlap was the mark of high-production values within the genre. Others had to do with issues of dispatching and rhythm: for example, how many words to use per panel, tier, page, or story, or the form that an optimal sequential arrangement might take. Still others dealt with the transcription of the soundtrack; strategic decisions had to be made regarding whether to keep or drop certain elements.

At first, each publisher tried to develop his own system, but there is general agreement that the model developed by Franco Bozzesi represents a decisive turning point in the history of the genre's typography. Bozzesi was not the first to launch film photonovel magazines, but the rules that he introduced turned his "classic" house style into an exemplary reference that all competitors either copied or deliberately differed from. Bozzesi's model for the interaction between word and image is the film photonovel's equivalent of Hollywood's continuity editing. In both cases, the rules of composition (Bozzesi) and montage (Hollywood) are incorporated so smoothly that one can (almost) forget that the final product results from a painstaking and complicated treatment of heterogeneous bits and pieces. Like all classic styles, the Bozzesi house style was the result of much hard work, although this effort was nearly invisible to the audience.

More concretely, the innovations introduced by the Bozzesi publications are evident in the main illustration on the first page of "La Piste des éléphants," the 1958 French version of *Elephant Walk* (William Dieterle, 1954, Paramount, starring Elizabeth Taylor, Dana Andrews, and Peter Finch), which can be described as follows (fig. 3.5):

- The creation of a powerful protocol for the opening panel and credits as well as the first narrative panel of the work: both panels systematically adopt a split-screen presentation. This anticipates the division of the textual tiers in two panels: the first peritextual panel is neatly divided in two parts (on the left, a picture of the protagonists, and on the right, a relatively large number of prestigious names and references); the second peritextual panel obeys the same compositional principle, as if it were divided by the spine of a book, and uses the same lettering style that appears in the credit panel, which facilitates the transition from peritext to text.
- The regular dispatching of the text over all panels, which produces a steady reading rhythm. The amount of text is large, but not discouragingly so, which allows the reader to pause and go back and forth between text and image.

FIGURE 3.5. *"La Piste des éléphants"* (Elephant Walk, *1954, William Dieterle),* Star Ciné Roman, *15 February 1958, p. 3.*

- The clear distinction between verbal levels: italicized all-caps for the narrator's voice, and roman upper- and lowercase letters for the dialogues, a model many readers may have known from comics.
- The prevention of possible overlap between words and images, which depends on the combination of two convergent codes: first, the visual "marginalization" of the text, which never occupies the center of the image, the formally and semantically most important and saturated area of the image in classic Hollywood cinema (Paul 2016); second, the rubbing out of the underlying part of the picture (see, for instance, the last panel of the opening page), or the enlargement of the image by the almost invisible addition of a section to the upper part of the panel. Often the transition between the rubbed-out part of the image and its continuation as background for the text is so skillfully done that one hardly notices the retouching.
- The combination of these even text zones with a page layout that is equally smooth: no sudden or rough transformations of the basic grid. The height of the tiers remains the same, and so does the width of the panels, more or less, yet never mechanically, in order to avoid boredom. The large size of the images (the dimensions of the magazine are comparable to those of present-day *Life* magazine) likewise helps maintain this impression of softness and balance.

The problem with the Bozzesi system is that it may have worked too well. After the initial creative chaos and uncertainty of the first attempts, it became the implicit model for the genre, and it could be routinely repeated for many years. A quick look at issues of the same magazine published five or six years later shows that the same model is still in place. The model, however, became somewhat lazy: the verbal elements expanded, and the effort to come up with more concise and transparent pages seemed to wane. It is apparent that in the first years, the Bozzesi team had to fight to create clarity, but once the protocol was solidly established, the creative attention seemed to relax and the whole system weakened. It simply survived, and eventually condemned itself by no longer changing in a rapidly changing market context.

The major change that the Bozzesi protocol manipulated from the beginning concerns the integration of set pictures (in principle, the Bozzesi magazines worked with copies of used-up film stills). These large pictures often occupy a double tier, sometimes even a full page, with a triple goal: they compensate for the lower quality of the small panels; they break the monotony of the three-by-two grid; and their focus on the movie stars introduces a kind of "poster effect" in the film photonovel, thus radically redefining its function. Instead of being part of an adapted filmic narrative, these set pictures became a catalogue or sample set of celebrity pictures that one could freely cut out and use decoratively or in other ways, as stated in the friendly advice given to the readers of the Spanish version of *The Nights of Cabiria* and indirectly confirmed by the absence of certain images, such as back-cover pictures or centerfolds, in extant film photonovels.

French publishers in the film-photonovel business often came from a double background. While some of them were new to the trade, most others had worked in photonovels or film novels. The next examples illustrate this twofold influence and examine how French newcomers tried to find satisfying ways to imitate without shallowly copying.

Photonovel publishers were the first to move into film photonovels. Les Éditions mondiales—the press group founded by Cino del Duca and famous for its flagship publication, the photonovel magazine *Nous Deux*—introduced its new take on the film photonovel in several market segments at the same time. Les Éditions mondiales proposed a restyling of its movie and celebrity magazine *Ciné-Révélation*, which was strongly indebted to the photonovel aesthetic and targeted a photonovel readership. In 1956 the magazine started including film photonovels but followed a policy aligned with the photonovel. Indeed, *Ciné-Révélation* was one of the rare magazines that serialized film photonovels, in order to experiment with them in a short-story format. This seemed like a logical step for a move to align the film photonovel with the photonovel, a medium defined by a mix of short stories and serializations. But a film photonovel was always published after the adapted movie's first run, so publication of complete versions immediately became the norm for the film-photonovel protocol. But magazines still dominated by the rules of photonovel publishing misunderstood this. Les Éditions mondiales launched a whole range of *Nous Deux* lookalikes in the film photonovel format, magazines that tried to cash in on the image and the prestige of the leading photonovel magazine while offering a new format and content, namely, a complete film in print. In addition to *Nous Deux Film*—the series that eventually emerged as the house's dominant film-photonovel magazine, surviving until 1962 (Ghera 2006)—Éditions mondiales also tried its luck with *Nous Deux présente: Aventures Actions* (1960?–1962?), *Nous Deux présente: Festival Film* (1956?–1961?), *Nous Deux présente: Film Moderne* (1957?–1959?), *Nous Deux présente: Roman Film Étoile* (1957?–1962?), *Nous Deux présente: Roman Film Série d'or* (1959?–1960?), *Nous Deux présente: Roman Film Vedette* (1959?–1964?), *Vie heureuse* (1958?–1963?), and *Mon amour* (1957?–1959?).[8]

The example that I will tackle here is Jean Cocteau's *Beauty and the Beast* (*La Belle et la Bête*, 1946, starring Jean Marais and Josette Day), an adaptation of the fairy tale as told by Jeanne-Marie Leprince de Beaumont in 1757. Most readers know at least the Disney version—this one is, of course, somewhat different. Like the Bozzesi series, *Nous Deux présente: Roman Film Vedette*, in which the film photonovel appeared, foregrounded prestigious and successful movies (*vedette* means "star" or "celeb"). One might even say that it drew much of its raison d'être from the typically French policy of transmedializing canonical literary works.[9] And this is what the film photonovel version of the Cocteau film did: it adapted a well-known part of the national heritage into a new medium that represented the latest fad. The canonical dimension of the publication is stressed by three other elements. First, the adapted film was not a recent one, contrary to usual practice, meaning that the publication purposely turned away from the present and went back to "the best that has been thought and said," in literature as well as in cinema.[10] Moreover, film, unlike literature, is not a medium that automatically reveals a split between elite and popular taste: Cocteau's movie was both critically acclaimed and well received at the box office. Canonical, here, is not in opposition to popular. Second, although the film was released before the formulation of auteur ideology, it is a superlative example of a collective work largely made by one man, the poet-director Jean Cocteau. Also critical to the final product was Henri Alekan, the man in charge of the fascinating cinematography and an equally well-respected artist in the French movie industry. The choice of the movie was, therefore, a handy way of espousing the new spirit of the times, that of the New Wave, or Left Bank, cinema, while not disheartening traditional audiences, which were more interested in actors than in directors or technicians. As we will see, the peritextual framing of the movie also goes in another, non-auteur-oriented direction. For *Nous Deux Vedette*, one could say that the film photonovel was a way of having its cake and eating it too. Finally, the movie as well as its adaptation strikes a strong nationalistic chord, yet the two do not follow the same path. Released in 1946 in the aftermath of collaboration and epuration, the film makes a strong claim for what "Frenchness" meant in the turmoil after World War II. Published in 1959, when the debate on French identity was taking different forms (Frey 2014) and Cocteau's attitudes during the war years (judged pro-German by many critics) had ceased to be an issue, the new adaptation can also be seen as an attempt to establish a domestic form of the Italian film-photonovel format.

The film-photonovel version of *Beauty and the Beast* must have met a knowing audience; there is no reason to doubt that the general public knew both the original story and the Cocteau movie well. But what happens in the adaptation? The first impression (also a lasting one) is that of a strange paradox, a flagrant contradiction even. The whole publication is manifestly intended to reflect the aesthetic and cultural ambition of Cocteau's film as well as to pay tribute to *Beauty and the Beast* in a popular format, the notion of national cultural heritage being the framework in which to reconcile elite and popular taste. The marketing mix of the film-photonovel version does not hide this upscale ambition: "Beauty and the Beast" was in the second issue of the new magazine *Nous Deux Vedette*; the cover image became a full-color poster of the male and female stars; and the large size of the magazine was reinforced by the standard story length. Fifty-nine pages are dedicated to the narrative, substantial for a magazine that generally featured shorter adaptations. The peritextual elements that accompany the story reject all lowbrow sections, such as celebrity gossip, advertisements for other publications of the publisher, movie news, and the like. Moreover, they exclusively focus on a "serious" presentation of the stars: Josette Day, whose face is prominent on the front cover, is presented on the inside front cover of the magazine; Jean Marais, the big star, is praised on the last page of the magazine; and there is some information on supporting actor Marcel André on the inside back cover.

The actual publication, however, is rather disappointing (see fig. 3.6). First—and here the idea of the knowing audience becomes extremely functional—the erasure of some artistic features of the movie is noticeable from the beginning. For example, the deletion of the credit sequence of the movie, an artistic sequence, is noteworthy because in the film it hints at the intermingling of writing and directing (a key issue in the auteur ideology), and because it performs a metalepsis, that is, an interpenetration of different narrative levels (Genette 2004), which is, in this case, a rhetorical and narrative device that aligns with the genre of the fairy tale and the extremely willing suspension of disbelief asked of adult readers and spectators. In the movie, a man immediately identifiable as the director (Cocteau was a public figure, and his face was certainly recognized by all spectators) writes the names of the two stars on a blackboard. Marais and Day then come to the fore—and even if we only see their backs, we understand who is who—to wipe out his or her name on the blackboard. Cocteau then writes down the title of the film and the name of the director, after which the rest of the credits appear on the blackboard. After these credits, the filmed peritext shows a technician giving the clap for the first take. The shooting seems to start, but then the images are interrupted for an authorial statement. After the first dialogue between technician and director (lines 1–4 in the quotation below), a text unfolds on screen:[11]

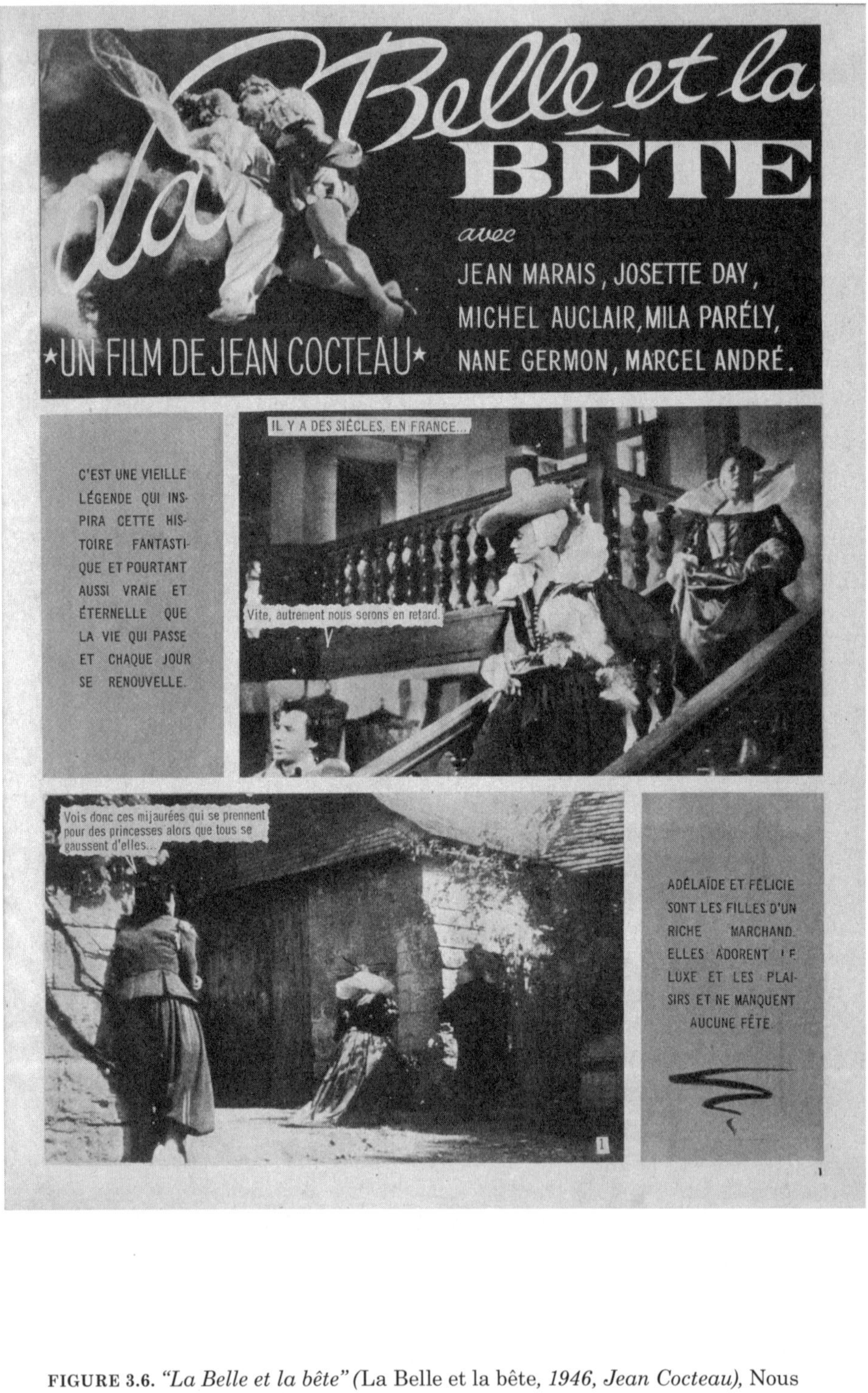

FIGURE 3.6. *"La Belle et la bête"* (La Belle et la bête, *1946, Jean Cocteau),* Nous Deux présente Roman Film Vedette, *April–June 1959, p. 3.*

Action.
Rolling.
Beauty and the Beast take one
Cut. Just a minute

Children believe what we tell them. They have complete faith in us. They believe that a rose plucked from a garden can plunge a family into conflict. They believe that the hands of a human beast will smoke when he slays a victim and this will cause the beast shame when a young maiden takes up residence in his home. They believe a thousand other simple things. I ask you a little of this childlike simplicity and to bring us luck let me speak four truly magic words, childhood's "open sesame": "Once upon a time . . ."

—JEAN COCTEAU

This original, functional peritextual transition completely disappears in the film-photonovel version, which reduces the contact zone between context and text, between (real) life and fictional world, to a banal opening text panel:

C'est une vieille légende qui inspira cette histoire fantastique et pourtant aussi vraie et éternelle que la vie qui passe et chaque jour se renouvelle.

[It is an old legend that inspired this story, which is fantastic yet as true and eternal as life, which passes away and renews itself day after day.]

In a similarly banal way, the "poetical" opening caption is immediately toned down by the first speech balloon in the same frame:

IL Y A DES SIÈCLES EN FRANCE.
Vite, autrement nous serons en retard.

[MANY CENTURIES AGO IN FRANCE.
Hurry up, or we will be late.]

This rather disappointing opening leaves next to nothing of the poetic and original start of the Cocteau movie; we then may be further dismayed when we read the captions and balloons and see how they are positioned in the panels and on the page. The first page displays a clear attempt to compose a well-balanced layout, with a simple but elegant chiasm between text panel and image panel (AB/BA). But this symmetry is disrupted by the rather chaotic inclusion of narrative captions and speech balloons. Moreover, everything is "ugly" in these verbal elements. The lettering does not match the image, contrary to the promise made by the first credit image on the page, in which one finds a smooth integration of the verbal and the visual. On the other hand, the size of these captions and balloons does not always have a meaningful relationship with the form and structure of the images on which they are superposed, and it is not always possible to see any pattern behind the way that these elements are added to the symmetrically built tiers. Granted, there are some examples of such a successful encounter between text and image (the double spread on pages 12–13 is far from unattractive), but many pages remain as chaotic as the first one. Finally, none of these verbal elements have any literary value. They are banal and poorly written, so much so that it is difficult to see them as the verbal counterpart of the visual and narrative ambitions of the movie that they represent—of which Cocteau had already published an original and well-written "making of" version (Baetens 2016). And what about the pictures themselves? To call them banal and badly printed is an understatement. Nothing remains of the magnificence of the visual effects obtained by the director of photography, Henry Alekan, and readers of the film photonovel may think that they are looking at a fifth-generation copy of a technically deficient original.

The rest of the work hardly helps ameliorate this impression of visual and textual poverty. One feels throughout that there is an attempt to supersede the overly transparent and somewhat boring protocol of the Bozzesi model, in which the image suffers from verbal overkill. One feels, as well, a similar effort to reject the type of photonovel based on the *Ciné-Révélation* model (an in-house model, since that magazine was also published by Les Éditions mondiales), but the result is rarely felicitous. There are well-made, sometimes stunning pages, but their effect is spoiled by clumsiness at other levels, in addition to the lack of a clear approach. A striking symptom of this ambivalence is the use of typographical ornaments often based on the cul-de-lampe, an inverted triangular form placed at the end of a passage of text. The Bozzesi model, as well as many other film-photonovel magazines, tends to use these elements as an aesthetic "filler" of text panels that would otherwise remain mostly empty. In "Beauty and the Beast," the use of ornaments is functional, not only typographically, but also thematically: they were frequently used in premodern typography and manuscripts and perfectly suit the "once upon a time" spirit of a fairy tale. The ornament at the bottom of the last text panel of page 1 is, therefore, easy to understand: it stresses the medieval atmosphere of the story, it introduces an element of variation in the rigid chiasm between the last two tiers of the page, and it creates a cliffhanger effect. Yet the following pages do not confirm this first, positive impression: it is difficult to discover a real method to the presence or absence of these ornaments, which, in addition, remain the same on all pages (actually, there are two of them, but the reasons behind their choice and alternation never become clear). This contrasts markedly with their use in other magazines, where one generally finds either a purely visual use of these typographical signs or a purposeful effort to adapt them to the specific narrative context. They seem to do more than just fill empty space in "Beauty and the Beast," but their repetition is, despite some superb counterexamples, often mechanical and superficial.

To conclude: the Cocteau adaptation is a good example of an ambivalent and transitional film-photonovel project. It tries to push the limits of the genre beyond the mere reuse of photonovel clichés—hence the emphasis on the visual dimension, along with the upscale narrative and cultural framing. But it does not propose a viable alternative to the streamlining that Bozzesi was proposing in the same years. Its attempt to invent new forms combining simplicity with complexity sometimes produces aesthetically pleasant and unobtrusive solutions, but generally speaking, the result remains clumsy and poor. Although apparently less ambitious in many regards, the model developed by the competing magazine *Mon Film* proved at least as efficient and convincing. I address the difference between the two French publications with the help of the adaptation of a resolutely contemporary and, to some extent, avant-garde work.

Moderato cantabile is, just like Cocteau's *Beauty and the Beast*, a work that enjoyed both popular success and later cult status. The novel, published in 1958, brought fame to its author, Marguerite Duras (1914–1996), a writer and director who was among the chief figures of French cultural life in the second half of the twentieth century. Just as the books by Duras helped establish the fame of the New Novel in the 1950s and 1960s, her cinematographic work—she was the scriptwriter for Alain Resnais's 1959 *Hiroshima, mon amour*,[12] coscriptwriter of Peter Brook's adaptation of *Moderato cantabile* in 1960, and, eventually, a film director herself—proved paramount to the emergence of New Wave cinema. The intertwining of film and literature in these years was almost complete, and no author blurred their boundaries as profoundly as Marguerite Duras. The film version of *Moderato cantabile* was a prestigious production with an impressive cast and crew (Jeanne Moreau and Jean-Pierre Belmondo were among the leading actors of the New Wave; Peter Brook worked as a director at the Royal Shakespeare Company; Duras had risen to worldwide fame with *Hiroshima, mon amour*) and a definitely modern, yet not experimental, look. Within the New Novel and the New Wave constellation, the position of Duras has always been distinct: first because of the overtly autobiographical aspects of her work in a decade, the 1950s, that defined modernism and the avant-garde as antisubjective (Robbe-Grillet [1963] 1989); and second, because of a pathetic, some would say pathological, emphasis on love, passion, and madness that the book intensifies in a typically dry and understated style. In content, Duras's stories, always a strange mix of the utterly banal and the most extreme sublime, have a clear link to the universe of the photonovel and, therefore, the film photonovel.

Moderato cantabile is a musical term that anecdotally refers to the piano lessons taken by the son of the story's heroine, Anne Desbarèdes, the wife of a rich factory owner whose neglect and emotional dullness bring her to despair. A passionate murder next to the apartment where the weekly piano lessons take place triggers a mad love affair between Anne and a man named Chauvin, a worker in her husband's factory, who was present during the murder and who tells Anne about it. It is an impossible affair, however, that ends with Chauvin leaving for another city and her going back to her husband and her son. The book and the film mainly comprise conversations between the two lovers in the bar where they meet during their walks in the neighborhood (see fig. 3.7). The theme is clichéd (David Lean's 1945 *Brief Encounter* follows the same pattern), yet the exceptionally simple but dense style of Duras gives the novel an almost mythic dimension. The film admirably captures this tension between utmost simplicity and extreme passion.

The film-photonovel version was produced by the magazine *Mon Film*, the major French competitor of *Nous Deux Film*. The genealogy of this magazine was, however, different from that of the magazines published by Les Éditions mondiales: its background was not that of the photonovel but of the film novel. Its policy was based on the following principles, which complete the traditional list of general genre features, such as melodramatization and a length of roughly fifty pages:

- An exclusive focus on French cinema, without any preference for a particular genre, but a strong link with celebrity and star culture. It was in *Mon Film* that one was most likely to find Brigitte Bardot's movie adaptations.
- The exclusive use of set pictures, which distinguished the magazine from its main competitors, which largely worked with material based on film stills. The visual advantages of this choice were clear, but it was a tricky policy narratively, since it often reduced the number of available photographs.

FIGURE 3.7. *"Moderato cantabile" (*Moderato Cantabile*, 1960, Peter Brook),* Mon Film, *December 1960, p. 50.*

- An extremely simple, absolutely legible, page layout, based on the nearly systematic use of a perfect grid (three identical tiers, each with two identically sized frames, except for the opening credit panel and some infrequent pages). This absence of variation might have betrayed a lack of aesthetic ambition, but it cannot be denied that this minimalist choice was functional and efficient and had the advantage of making the film photonovel a transparent window onto the movie. Even if the format of the film frame was not the same as that of the set pictures, it was a format that remained the same from the first until the last image of the work.
- An attempt to produce maximal readability of captions and speech balloons, which were generally short, clearly distinguished, hand lettered, and superposed on the image even though all of them were printed on a white rectangle.
- A sober and unashamedly commercial take on the niche market. *Mon Film* published the film of the month (although it took some time before the adequate periodicity was defined), with relatively few peritextual accompaniments other than advertisements for the other issues of the series and very lowbrow advertisements for the happiness of "body and mind."

All these principles can be found in the adaptation of the Peter Brook movie. As with Cocteau and "Beauty and the Beast," it is implausible to assume that the *Mon Film* version was authored—or even authorized—by Marguerite Duras. The changes made to the dialogue and narrative comments are often drastic, the writing does not sound Durasian (it sounds as it is supposed to in a film photonovel), and the permanent tension between the ordinary and the sublime, a typical feature of the Durasian style, is not always prominent. The adaptation works well despite the flattening of the verbal elements, the melodramatic overwriting of the story, and the erasure of the "universal" character of Duras's story, which, for example, refrains from giving too many geographic indications by explicitly situating the time, place, and characters.

The positive impression made by this film photonovel results from the correspondence between, on the one hand, the general rules of the relationship between word and image as fixed by the *Mon Film* protocol and, on the other, the idiosyncrasies of Duras's minimalist style (minimalist in its verbal and narrative features, maximalist in its readerly impact). The form and content of the verbal and narrative layers of book and film are somewhat watered down, but the visual architecture of the film-photonovel version remains simple, sound, straight.[13] The captions and balloons do not harm the images, despite the resizing of the wide-screen movie images to fit the square ratio of the set pictures. The visual organization of the pages is consistently readable but never rigid, thanks to the diversification of the grid by the varied length of the captions and balloons. The differing uses of these elements underscore the mood of Anne Desbarèdes and the changes that she experiences when going back to her husband.

With *Cow Boy Magazine* (1964–1968), published by Ponzoni, a lowbrow competitor of Bozzesi, the history of the interaction between word and image in the film photonovel may seem as if it came to an end. "Arizona" was the second issue of a very cheap western series that represented a transition for the vanishing, traditional film novel, which targeted readers of women's magazines, and a regression to small niche markets that were sometimes underground (science fiction, westerns, horror, and, eventually, porn). *Cow Boy* and many other small-format magazines of these years—the small format (16 cm × 18.5 cm, or 6.3 in × 7.3 in, and sometimes even smaller [Capart 2015]) being itself a direct sign of diminished prestige—increasingly recycled the US western corpus, but it is not always easy to identify the origin of the material. "Arizona," for instance, is uncredited, although one might think that the female character on the front cover was sufficiently recognizable to the target audience, as was the figure of John Wayne on the cover of the first issue of *Cow Boy Magazine*. And the savage reuse and endless recycling of all kinds of images in several publications was a staple feature of the small western magazines of the period (one of the usual suspects was Clint Eastwood, then immensely popular in Europe thanks to the CBS serial *Rawhide*). Apparently, readers did not pay attention to the fact that the actors highlighted on the cover were absent from the film photonovel, and the same can be said of the recurrent use of certain frames in various narratives. Another sign of the times is the erosion of any meaningful relationship between text and peritext (fig. 3.8): in "Arizona," the film photonovel is completed by a western short story, but the inside pages of the front and back covers also contain the serialization of a sci-fi story, which begins out of the blue (it is specified that we are reading "the continuation of previous chapters," but no information on the story is provided) and ends no less abruptly ("to be continued").

"Arizona" is still a film photonovel, however, and even a typical one, although a completely ossified and degenerated example of the genre. A look at the work shows that "Arizona" expands on the Bozzesi model, but more mechanically than earlier styles. We recognize the grid, the neat separation of text and image, and the tendency, typical of many "late" film photonovels, to include more and more text. Perhaps it was cheaper to produce these highly conventional chunks of text first rather than to start

FIGURE 3.8. *"Arizona" (original unknown),* Cow Boy Magazine, *February 1966, p. 24.*

by carefully watching the film in order to choose the most appropriate film stills, which are reprinted in a way that make them almost illegible. In "Arizona," the captions and dialogue consume up to 50 percent of the available space. But much more is going on. The most striking aspects of "Arizona" are not only the crude discrepancy between the supreme readability of the text and the sometimes indistinguishable images but also the radical shift in the relationship between text and images. The latter are purely illustrative, and their function is generic: they carefully avoid any tension between text and image and they proclaim that we are reading a western, nothing less and nothing more. The images do nothing to compose a page or contribute to the telling of the story. They are there to provide the reader with a genre marker and to insist on the fact that the story is based on a movie, which gives it some street credibility with the intended readership (male adolescents?).

In other words, "Arizona" is a magazine that offers 50 percent text and 50 percent images, but that is, in practice, 100 percent telling: the showing just frames the telling. One does not have to look at the images to follow the story, and a close look at them proves unsatisfactory: besides ceaselessly reminding us of all possible genre stereotypes, they hardly contribute to the narrative. Visually, they often look weird, as if the characters had been cut out from other pictures and then glued onto a new background (a photographic technique popular in publicity photography during the period). This technique may also hint at the fact that the images in "Arizona" do not originate form one source, the movie called *Arizona* (?), but are a remix of stills borrowed from an informal western-movies archive.

To briefly conclude: word and image, telling and showing, are key features of film-photonovel poetics, but an analysis of them shows that it is not possible to isolate them from other, no less important, aspects, such as page layout and the representation of action and body movements. The following chapters address these aspects and, whenever necessary, return to the fundamental relationships between the verbal and the visual.

4 / Clear Grids, Blurred Lines

Issues of page layout have always been key to the study of graphic narratives. For this reason, the literature on page and panel composition in comics and photonovel studies is wide-ranging. All major critics have written extensively on the subject, and nearly all handbooks have a chapter on the topic. The emergence and institutionalization of comics studies, for instance, are fundamentally indebted to one or more of the following: the successful treatment of problems related to the dichotomy between linearity and tabularity (Fresnault-Deruelle 1976); the tension between narrative development and visual tableau (Peeters [1988] 2007; Peeters also developed a sophisticated taxonomy of their intertwining); the intricate relationships between breakdown and closure, that is, between the division of the narrative into single panels and the readerly effort to bridge the gap between these panels (Hatfield 2005); and the readerly experience of discreet versus ostentatious page layouts (Groensteen [1999] 2009). All these notions and concepts offer a better understanding of the dialectic play of decomposition and recomposition in sequentially arranged narratives told with the help of fixed, verbally enhanced images. There are, however, a certain number of pitfalls in the transfer of reading methods for comics and photonovels to the less-studied domain of the film photonovel. It is crucial to address these potential missteps as we work to establish appropriate reading frames that accurately assess the genre under scrutiny.

Why Film and Comics Models Fall Short

The most pertinent concern is that of the limits posed by any tight comparison between the film photonovel and the genres that surround it. Film is the easiest case to address, for although the montage principles of cinema seem a good model for the analysis of page layout in the film photonovel, the comparison falls short. Granted, the latter includes many illustrations of all the major montage principles of the former: alternate scenes, establishing shots followed by subjective frames, shot and reverse shots in panels of dialogue, and so forth. But we should focus, first, on the differences between the two media, which are not limited merely to the shift from moving to fixed images (a difference that more and more scholars tend to challenge; see Hoelzl and Marie 2015). To start, there is the difference between the single image of the film (we see one image at a time, except in split-screen or multiple-screen projections, which are hardly represented in the traditional, single-screen feature cinema that is the primary resource of the film photonovel) and the juxtaposition of several pictures on the pages of a film photonovel, which can be seen at the same time (single-image pages are represented in the corpus, but they are never the default option in the type of mass-media film photonovel analyzed in this book). The consequences of this simple distinction are vital. In a movie, the combination of single images is temporally arranged: its key principle is that of succession (one image after another). In a film photonovel, the combination is temporally as well as spatially arranged: the panels not only are temporally combined—we are intended to read the images in a certain order as the narrative unfolds on the page—but also obey a purely visual logic of juxtaposition. This more complex organization produces a special tension between time and space, that is, between panel-to-panel transitions, on the one hand, and tabularity, or overall visual perception, on the other. We read sequentially (first this image, then that one), and we look globally (we see the image that we are reading and the rest of the page or part of the page—depending, for instance, on the number of images on the page and their internal structure—at the same time).

A second set of differences that distinguish film (the adapted work) from the film photonovel (the adapting work) occurs at the level of the images projected on screen and on the page display. Contrary to common assumptions, most pictures in a film photonovel are *not* those that were shown in the theater. Most of them were recropped, to start—a very noticeable intervention in this period of triumphant wide-screen technology. In certain cases, their print quality is so poor that it is difficult to recognize the original. Sometimes the film photonovel uses set pictures instead of film stills, and these pictures can differ radically from what we see in the movie. They summarize certain gestures or scenes, isolate the actors and actresses following the logic of celebrity photography, and evoke passages that did not survive the final cut (Jacobs 2010). And finally, the film's spectator sees "only images" (at least in principle, for the rest of the theater is meant to be dark and thus invisible), whereas the reader of a film photonovel perceives more than the images that are verbally enhanced (few films from the period were subtitled, and to hear a voice-over is not the same as to read a narrative caption or text panel). The reader of the film photonovel sees the gutters as well as the surrounding images and margins of the page, which all serve as a kind of supplementary frame (Peeters 1991). And in most cases, the reader is privy to the "real world" (of which the film-photonovel magazine as a material object is only a small slice). All these elements have an impact on the status as well as the perception of page-layout questions.

The comparison with comics and photonovels, which share quite a few features—for example, their page layouts—seems logical. But crucial differences are readily apparent. At a narrative level, the most striking dissimilarity has to do with the shift from serialization to complete story publication. An heir to nineteenth-century melodramas, the basic unit of the photonovel is less the story or the page than the installment (with an average length of four to six pages). Each week, the photonovel unfolded a new fragment of a larger story, which the reader explored at two levels, first as part of a larger chain (which is summarized at the beginning of each installment and reframed or reopened at the end with the help of suspense and cliffhanger mechanisms), and second as an independent whole (a kind of micronarrative). Conversely, the film photonovel was published as a complete story (the few, short-lived exceptions occurring in the early days of the genre, when the film photonovel had not yet been dissociated from the photonovel). Moreover, the stories told are familiar to the reader; even those who had not seen an adapted movie would have heard about it or might have known the plot from trailers, reviews, reportages, word of mouth, and so on.

The consequences of this shift are substantial. They imply a weaker, more segmented succession of pages and sections than is seen in the photonovel, since the film photonovel does not have the same stop-and-go dynamic of fragments that are required to create and maintain a permanent tension in order to make sure that the reader will "come and see next week," that is, buy the new installment. But they may also imply, and this is less visible, a different status of the page and thus the page layout. Compared with the photonovel, the film photonovel provides more room to construe the page as an independent visual structure, regardless of the role that it plays in keeping the narrative tension alive. In other words, since the basic aim of the film photonovel is not just to retell a story but also to offer a visual trace of the movie and its actors and actresses, the absence of the installment technique puts less pressure on the panel-to-panel and page-to-page transitions and the narrative tension that results from them, and allows for a stronger, yet never exclusive, take on tabularity and visual composition. The relative lack of cliffhangers in the film photonovel is one of the logical consequences of this move.

In Praise of Constraint

A second pitfall is the idea that film photonovels have the same freedom and creative opportunities that the makers of a comic or a movie enjoy. It is now commonly accepted that artistic freedom, certainly in the cultural industries field (of which the film photonovel is a part), is relative. Symbol producers, as authors working in the cultural industries are called (Hesmondhalgh 2013), have a large degree of freedom in creating the form and content of their work, but they are bound by numerous production or institutional constraints, which Richard A. Peterson (1982) has classified in five fields: law, technology, market, organizational structure, and occupational careers. On top of these constraints, the film photonovel is also burdened by two others whose weight can be felt throughout any work.

The first one has already been addressed. It is the all-pervading influence of the house style of the magazine, that is, the editorial voice, which does not allow for much internal variation. Even if work on a film photonovel did not take place in a studio, the editor of each magazine transmitted strict specifications to the symbol producers who built the work, as can be inferred from the strong homogeneity within each series. Even in series that strive for a different look and feel, there is always an underlying formula that was followed. *Amor Film* magazine, for instance, is probably the series that attempted to diverge most radically from any known layout or narrative film-photonovel model. It poured out issues that all obeyed exactly the same divergent model. To a certain extent, the heterodox formula of *Amor Film* was even more repetitive and monotonous than that of the most unimaginative of its competitors, since its unusual page layout was obstinately implemented on each page, making the *Amor*

Film scheme the most predictable one among all film photonovels. *Amor Film* is often dismissed as "crazy" and "incomprehensible," but much more method than madness defined its take on the medium.

The constraint that shaped the film photonovel the most was the necessity of reusing a limited set of pictures to tell a story whose plot could not be altered, along with the impossibility of supplementing this set with new images. When film photonovels reused film stills, this was a problem that remained theoretical, at least at first sight. But when only set pictures were available (or when the material quality of the film stills was so poor that set pictures had to be used), it becomes a real issue. Often, there were simply not enough images, and those available did not necessarily cover all elements of the plot. Ironically, the quantitative problem of an insufficient number of images was more detrimental in film photonovels based on film stills than in works based on set pictures. Indeed, the latter generally succeeded in finding subtle solutions to the lack of pictures, whereas the former struggled to deal with film stills whose quality was so poor that they had to be supplemented with set pictures. This enrichment was far from neutral. The temptation to reprint set pictures in a large format, often as full-page images, has disturbing effects on the rest of the work. Set pictures generally look posed, and their use disrupted the sense conveyed by more dynamic film-still pictures. Moreover, the combination of single-image pages and grid-structured pages was not always harmonious, not to mention the aesthetic clash between "beautiful" set pictures and "ugly" film frames. By remediating the flaws of works that drew only on film stills, the insertion of set pictures made these flaws even more visible, and not all film photonovels successfully negotiated the potential friction between the two types of images and the two types of page layouts.

Inside the Grid

Finally, it is necessary to stress that page layout cannot be analyzed in purely formal, mechanical terms; that is, as the mere result of the juxtaposition of a certain number of frames arranged in a certain number of tiers and having a certain width and height. The message conveyed by a symmetrically structured three-by-two grid (the basic formula followed by a subtle magazine such as *Mon Film*) contrasts strongly with the apparent chaos seen in the overlapping frames of *Amor Film* (the fiercest example of the antigrid formula). Page layout structures and meanings cannot be reduced to questions of panel size and place: they have relationships to other elements, such as elements added to the panels in the form of captions and speech balloons, as well as to the internal content and visual form of each framed image. A three-by-two grid detailing six successive steps in the same action is not comparable to a similar grid structure hosting a chromatically differentiated shot-reverse-shot sequence that alternates a woman in black and a man in white against the same background, or to one that goes back and forth between similar characters seen against varying backgrounds. In both instances, the grid might be identical, but the reader's visual experience of each is substantially different. A medium-specific approach to the study of the film photonovel must prioritize the interplay between formal page layout and the visual experiences of the work.

Readability: From Grid to Page and Back Again

It does not suffice to underline the special status of the three-by-two grid as the implicit or explicit model of all page-layout formulas in the film photonovel, since any emphasis on this constraint runs the risk of triviality. The grid is simply a given, and what matters most is how the grid is used in the overall strategy of page and story composition.

The fundamental concern of most magazines was to achieve a solid mix of simplicity and diversity. A good page layout avoids useless complications while offering sufficient variety—and variety does not necessarily imply the abandonment of the formal three-by-two grid. In fact, both these elements, simplicity and diversity, raise various issues of readability (Ricardou 1988). Readability, in the technical sense of the term, refers to the ease with which the reader is able to access and decipher the product: a readable page layout smoothly guides the eye of the reader from one panel to another. Psychologically, readability refers to visual and narrative pleasure: a readable page layout displays panel transitions as well as an overall look and feel that is aesthetically pleasing in its own right.

Psychological readability combines two chief elements: the aesthetic qualities of the image itself, including those of the represented subject (the beautiful actor or actress), and a well-balanced mixture of repetition and transformation. Pleasure can be found in a certain degree of chaos and surprise, or in monotony and minimalism, but a popular-fiction genre like the film photonovel refrains from formal excesses. It rejects both baroque and stripped-down compositions while trying to control variation. Such sufficient variation appears, symmetrically, at other levels, too. In this regard, the methodical reuse of the grid becomes logical: the very form of a simple grid, that is, a grid with a limited number of regular tiles, organizes the page in a way that never jeopardizes technical readability yet offers countless opportunities for diversity and variation, either by small changes in the tile structure or via the internal diversity of each tile.

The essential concern for readability helps explain the apparent monotony of the page layout of the film photonovel and the systematic attempts to include slight variations on it. It is crucial to stress the intermingling of these two aspects. Without the all-pervading grid, special page layouts could result in a loss of readability. This was a permanent fear for the makers of any film photonovel, which targeted a reader who was generally distracted or unprepared—hence the voice-over, the frequent redundancy of word and image, the overlap between telling and showing, the systematic averting of narrative ellipsis and cognitive gaps, and the like. But, without the ability to introduce variants, the standard grid would become asphyxiating, as clearly shown by *Mon Film*, which rarely deviated from the three-by-two grid structure. By choosing this grid as its default option, *Mon Film* efficiently solved the issue of technical readability. At the same time, it gained maximal effectiveness for the small changes introduced from panel to panel and from page to page, since these small differences were immediately recognizable. Although the absolute distinction between technical and psychological readability is impossible to maintain at a practical level, it provides a useful frame for organizing the ways in which the film photonovel explored and eventually systematized some medium-specific layout types.

In general, the film photonovel is "easy reading" (which does not necessarily mean fast reading), but once in a while obstacles hinder the decoding of its words and images. A brief description of these obstacles will provide a solid foundation for exploring the technical pros and cons of readability. Two major elements stand out: the film photonovel is a medium that prefers less to more. Too many images (per page), too many words (either on the image or next to it), too many gaps between images and words, are disturbances. Reading is more fluent when the number of images is reduced, the number of verbal inserts is limited (and not too fragmented), and the link between verbal and visual information is unproblematic. This purely quantitative caution also concerns the size of the elements. The film photonovel does not favor small images, and it tries to avoid small and unclear lettering. Qualitatively, the film photonovel prefers transparent relationships between words and images, even at the cost of redundancy. Gaps or unconventional arrangements tend to be avoided. Panels or sequence structures that compel the reader to supply a missing link between word and image are rare, since they disrupt the traditional reading order (left to right, then top to bottom). It is not surprising that the analysis of *Amor Film* discloses some infelicities. This drive for clarity does not, however, exclude the subtle interventions that make the page layout meaningful in itself. Since most works have a limited number of pictures per page, the juxtaposition of two images is full of possible meanings. In the short-story version of *Elevator to the Gallows* (*Ascenseur pour l'échafaud*, Louis Malle, 1958), for instance, the film photonovel gathers two characters—whose relationship is not clarified at first, but who eventually appear as the two murderers in the story—in the same tier. Here, the layout formally anticipates the plot structure: it works as a spoiler for the clever reader drawn to the teasing effects of these types of cues.

More interesting, however, are the technical conditions of psychological readability: that is, of the mechanisms that introduce variety without provoking disorder. From this point of view, the film photonovel frequently experiments with some interesting layout formulas that are different from what can be found in comics and photonovels.

The interventions related to panel-to-panel transitions concern the modulations of "centrifugal" and "centripetal" sequences. Given the importance of dialogue in the adapted films and the possible boredom of mechanically coupling shot-reverse-shot pictures in several successive tiers, the film photonovel uses elaborate montage techniques that bring variety to these tiers of two pictures. Instead of repeating images in which the characters are shown as looking at each other in the same way during the same verbal or visual exchange, the film photonovel breaks conventional eyeline matches. It combines or alternates "centripetal" pictures (character A in the left image of the tier looks to character B, virtually at the right side of the scene, whereas character B in the right image looks to the left, that is, to character A) with "centrifugal" pictures (which obey the opposite logic—A looks to the left while B is supposed to be on the right, and B looks to the right while A is supposed to be on the left; see fig. 4.1, in which there is an explicit contradiction between the direction of the gazes and the text stating that "she turns toward him"). The difference between the two types is aesthetically disruptive, thanks to the variety it introduces, but in many cases the film photonovel succeeds in making these changes evocative, as is true in *Moderato cantabile*.

At the level of page layout (that is, the interactions between panel-to-panel transitions), the film photonovel is marked by three major innovations. Since the number of images is generally limited, and since most of the images happen to have similar content, the film photonovel invented simple, reproducible mechanisms that work to avoid monotony. The most frequently used technique is that of the "divergent corner" (fig. 4.2). In this case, either the first or the last picture on the page breaks the visual homogeneity of the rest of the page, yet never so much that a completely new image is introduced. Since there is no need to maintain suspense, the task of the page layout is to softly nuance the otherwise exaggerated global

FIGURE 4.1. *"L'Amant fantôme" (*Pandora and the Flying Dutchman*, 1951, Albert Lewin),* Photo Roman*, February 1959, p. 20.*

FIGURE 4.2. *"Cœurs en détresse" (*El Indiano, *1955, Fernando Soler),* Miroir du cœur, *September 1959, p. 58.*

symmetry of the page—often a bending of the same image in the case of an ongoing action, or a checkerboard composition in the case of a dialogue.

This "divergent corner" technique has to show visually that the page is not a complete narrative unity but part of a larger whole. It also bridges the gap between two pages whose corners are structured along the lines of such a visual rhyme.

Finally, but still at page level, the film photonovel introduces a fascinating yet unobtrusive variation on the interplay between linearity and tabularity. In certain cases, the panel-to-panel transition does not follow the usual order from left to right, but from top to bottom. The reading is then organized as a vertical structure in columns, which one follows by starting from the left and moving right (layouts consisting of more than two columns are not attested to in the corpus). At first sight, such a layout seems disruptive of the traditional reading mode and thus violates the criterion of simplicity. This is, however, not the case, and the following example (fig. 4.3) summarizes the elements that are mobilized to compensate for the initial lack of classic linearity.[1]

Taken from *Pane, amore, e . . .* (*Scandal in Sorrento*, 1955, Dino Risi), the scene displays a stereotypical plot unit: the secret meeting of the lovers, who will eventually go their separate ways to find true love (or not)—indeed, this is what the whole film is about. Thanks to the strong visual differences between the two internally homogeneous columns, each layout column appears almost as an independent page. It is possible to read them naturally in an order that is in principle not "natural" at all. On the left, the sequence zooms in on character A, who approaches the scene of the amorous encounter. On the right, we see three close-ups of the leading actors—the images perfectly interchangeable, hence strongly dechronologized—whose impossible love affair is the heart of the story. The unequal distribution of the verbal information—there is little to read on the left, the characters becoming typically talkative once they start kissing—confirms the split between the two columns, which justifies the reading of the page in a way that, though unconventional, is typical of the spatial aesthetics of film photonovels. In this sense, the tabular composition of the whole paradoxically strengthens the linear decoding of the images.

The specific layout mechanisms of this page can be highlighted by a comparison with the two French versions of the same film photonovel, the first published by Franco Bozzesi (*Star Ciné Roman*, 15 March 1961; fig. 4.4) and the second by Arturo Mercurio one year later (*Ciné Sélection*, September 1962; fig. 4.5). Neither French version follows the original layout, which is replaced in both cases by a very banal and utterly linear page composition.

FIGURE 4.3. *"Pane, amore e . . ." (*Pane, amore e . . . *, 1955, Dino Risi); in Giovanni Fiorentino,* Luci del Sud: Sorrento un set per Sofia *(1995), p. 78.*

FIGURE 4.4. *"Pain, amour, ainsi soit-il" (*Pane, amore e . . . *, 1955, Dino Risi),* Star Ciné Roman*, 15 March 1961, p. 34.*

FIGURE 4.5. *"Pain, amour et . . ." (*Pane, amore e . . . , *1955, Dino Risi),* Ciné Sélection, *September 1962, p. 34.*

In the succession of the pages throughout the work, the film photonovel confirms what is observed at the level of page composition and in the panel-to-panel transitions. The key problem can be formulated this way: in a film photonovel that does not replicate the basic three-by-two grid page after page, how can one introduce changes that circumvent arbitrariness and visual unease? In other words: how can one make layout changes significant without resorting to gratuitous shock effects? The answer is twofold. First, it is important to make layout changes sparingly: the rarer they are, the easier it becomes to highlight their importance for the story. Second, when the narrative motivation is not obvious, a change in layout pattern should foreground an image of the actors and actresses as stars. Full-page images, for instance, should be comparable to celebrity inserts, not unlike the pinup centerfolds that the film photonovel regularly offered their readers, or to the back-cover color pictures that readers were invited to cut out and repurpose as posters. Other uses of divergent layout structures—for instance, erratic transformations or large pictures that do not focus on the stars—were designed to tickle the reader, since disruptions, large or small, of a given order inevitably produce a brief aesthetic charge, although it is difficult to push them beyond the purely visual level. The necessity to keep things simple required the film photonovel to not indulge too much in these kinds of experiments.

House Styles Strong and Weak: *Nous Deux Film*

The general analysis of layout procedures and policies lays bare a creative tension between a wide range of medium-specific preferences—the ways in which the film photonovel uses an underlying grid, something it shares with comics and photonovels, among others—and the pressure of each magazine's house style. In some cases, this style was inflexible, and in other cases, some degree of internal diversity was possible. The works chosen for close reading in the rest of this chapter were selected to cover a range of publishers and representative examples. The samples analyzed highlight the full spectrum of the corpus: upscale and lowbrow versions, French works and imported works, and film photonovels based on film stills and on set pictures.

After defining a formula, most magazines and publishers stuck to it loyally. Some publishers clearly believed in the commercial and artistic value of their products, but mere conservatism or a lack of openness could have been at work in companies organized from the top down. But it becomes clear that the house style was far from an ironclad rule, and other publishers and magazines with recognizable profiles were much more elastic in their approach, eager to accommodate both the personal taste of the subcontractors who made the photonovel and the singular demands of the adapted movie.

Nous Deux Film was a typical example of a publication with a multifaceted profile. Although the magazine was clearly distinguishable from other major players in the field, the difference was mainly "negative," in the sense that it refrained from simply doing what its competitors were proposing, but without elaborating a real model of its own. Unlike its principal challengers, such as the French *Mon Film* or the Italy-based production lines from Bozzesi (the market leader, even in France) and Ponzoni (its "cheaper" challenger), *Nous Deux Film*, which started in 1956 and ended in 1962 (Ghera 2006), differentiated itself by its lack of a strict layout style. It rather opaquely combined different approaches, all of them variations of the classic three-by-two grid and all indebted to the Bozzesi model (in their word-and-image relationships). There is, for instance, no direct link between page layout and movie type, just as there is no visible connection between page layout and verbal elements such as the architecture of the text panels or the narrative captions and speech balloons, which add a second grid to that of the image tiles.

The reason for this heterogeneity was mainly economic. An imprint of the *Nous Deux* empire, *Nous Deux Film* followed the business model of Les Éditions mondiales, a company always attentive to product diversification. After the introduction of the drawn novel in France, which he pioneered, Cino Del Duca slowly, almost reluctantly incorporated the photonovel in his publications. But the interest of Les Éditions mondiales in the new genre quickly became both lively and diffuse. The company was among the first to copy the new Italian import—the first "French" Bozzesi photonovels disembarked in 1956—and at the same time, Del Duca, who was in direct contact with the Italian market, started publishing film photonovels as well. Del Duca seemed not to target the new and specific audience of movie fans, but the much broader audience, well known and efficiently marketed to, that was buying great numbers of photonovel and drawn-novel magazines such as *Nous Deux*, the premier seller at newsstands of the 1950s. Via another one of its magazines, *Ciné-Révélation*, Les Éditions mondiales launched a film-photonovel format that was more a remediation of the photonovel than a supersession by a new medium. *Ciné-Révélation* published serialized film photonovels in a visual and narrative style that recalled the language of the photonovel, as if Del Duca did not want to make a real choice between photonovels and film photonovels. The more upscale format of *Nous Deux Film*, which was supposed to be a more medium-specific take on the film photonovel, bore the traces of a similar hesitation. Indeed, Les Éditions mondiales introduced not just one complete-story series but a whole assortment of magazines whose identities remain unclear. No fewer than nine series were published more or less simultaneously in the years 1956–1964, some of them rather short-lived and only sporadically published.

These magazines seemed to promise something special, but the promise fell short. Quite rapidly, *Nous Deux Film* emerged as the flagship publication of the house, where it acted as a substitute for the complete-story reprints of the drawn-novel serials, which were on their way out. Whereas the photonovels were never reprinted as separate issues (not even in the case of great commercial success), Les Éditions mondiales had a modest policy of reprinting some of its drawn-novels serials. *Nous Deux Film* tried to streamline the publisher's production in the field of the film photonovel but proved incapable of forging a strong editorial identity beyond the commercial patronage of *Nous Deux*, the photonovel magazine.

A brief comparison of two film photonovels published by the magazine, selected because they follow the same treatment of the verbal layer, shows how *Nous Deux Film* worked to implement innovations or characteristics less familiar, or unknown, to competing magazines. This comparison highlights the limits that the publisher encountered in its effort to customize existing models.

Readers of "La Loi" ("The Law"), the 1959 *Nous Deux Film* adaptation of a Franco-Italian movie from the same year based on a 1957 novel by Roger Vailland, might have been intrigued by the choice of this work by *Nous Deux Film*. While the magazine did not have a strict selection policy for the movies that it adapted, it typically showed no interest in politically risky themes (the core business of the Del Duca magazines was always romance), yet *The Law* was such a movie. The adapted author, Roger Vailland, was a well-known novelist, and his book, the winner of the most prestigious literary prize in France (the Prix Goncourt), reflected the profound disenchantment of a fellow traveler from the French Communist Party after revelations in 1953 of Stalin's dictatorship and the Soviet invasion of Hungary in 1956.[2] The "law" is the name of an illegal game played in rural Italy that metaphorizes the abysmal ferocity of class antagonism, social abuse, and the inextinguishable thirst for evil that lives in all of us and cruelly opposes the lust for life of each new generation. The younger generation is represented by Gina Lollobrigida, whose presence in the movie is the reason for the film photonovel.

As seen through the lens of *Nous Deux Film*, "The Law" is less a film-photonovel adaptation of the movie's watered-down version of Vailland's story than a pure star vehicle that hollows out the format of the film photonovel. The goal was to present readers with an endless series of pictures of Gina Lollobrigida, one of the sexiest actresses of the era, generally in close-up and sometimes in a risqué outfit. More than half of the photographs (101 out of 188, in a work of thirty-two pages) are pictures of the lead actress, and each of them appears as a variation of the full-color celebrity photograph that adorns the front cover. The layout principles of "The Law" reflect this tension between the film photonovel and the underlying medium of star photography. Most pages of the work show a playful transformation of the basic grid, but the result is always the same: a foregrounding of the importance of Gina Lollobrigida. The traditional balance of each tier between left and right as well as between the top, center, and bottom of the page is abandoned. The default option of the film photonovel is to introduce limited variations on this overall symmetry. In "The Law," however, one finds an explosion of unconventional compositions, both horizontally and vertically. To this infringement, one should add a second technique that distinguishes *Nous Deux Film*, even if it is not applied systematically: the use of "cut out" photographs (cropped-framed), that follow the curved contours of their key subjects (Lollobrigida in this case; see fig. 4.6).

The excessive use of different text types (special panels, captions, and dialogues, all with their own typography and space) exacerbates the visual chaos without contributing to a better understanding of the story. The plot is difficult to follow because of the relative shortness of the work, which is a typical feature of *Nous Deux Film*—a publication that never severed its ties to the world of women's magazines and their rich mix of different sections and items. We see this, for example, in movie news and celebrity gossip. Besides blurring the deeper political layers of the source novel, already softened in the movie adaptation, "The Law" does not prioritize issues of readability. It would be incorrect, however, to conclude that the layout or the general spirit of this adaptation is gratuitous. The visual disorder and narrative capriciousness reinforce the shift from film photonovel to something else—in this case, celebrity culture and photography. The general history of the medium makes evident that the film photonovel is a hybrid format, which "The Law" appropriates in order to profit from the genre.

The 1961 *Nous Deux Film* version of *La Chartreuse de Parme* (*The Charterhouse of Parma*), the famous nineteenth-century novel by Stendhal, adapted for the screen by Christian-Jacque in 1948, looks quite different. As in the case of *Beauty and the Beast*, it is an example of the upscale aspirations of the magazine, which tried not only to cash in on recent releases but also to attach the name of the magazine to the national cultural

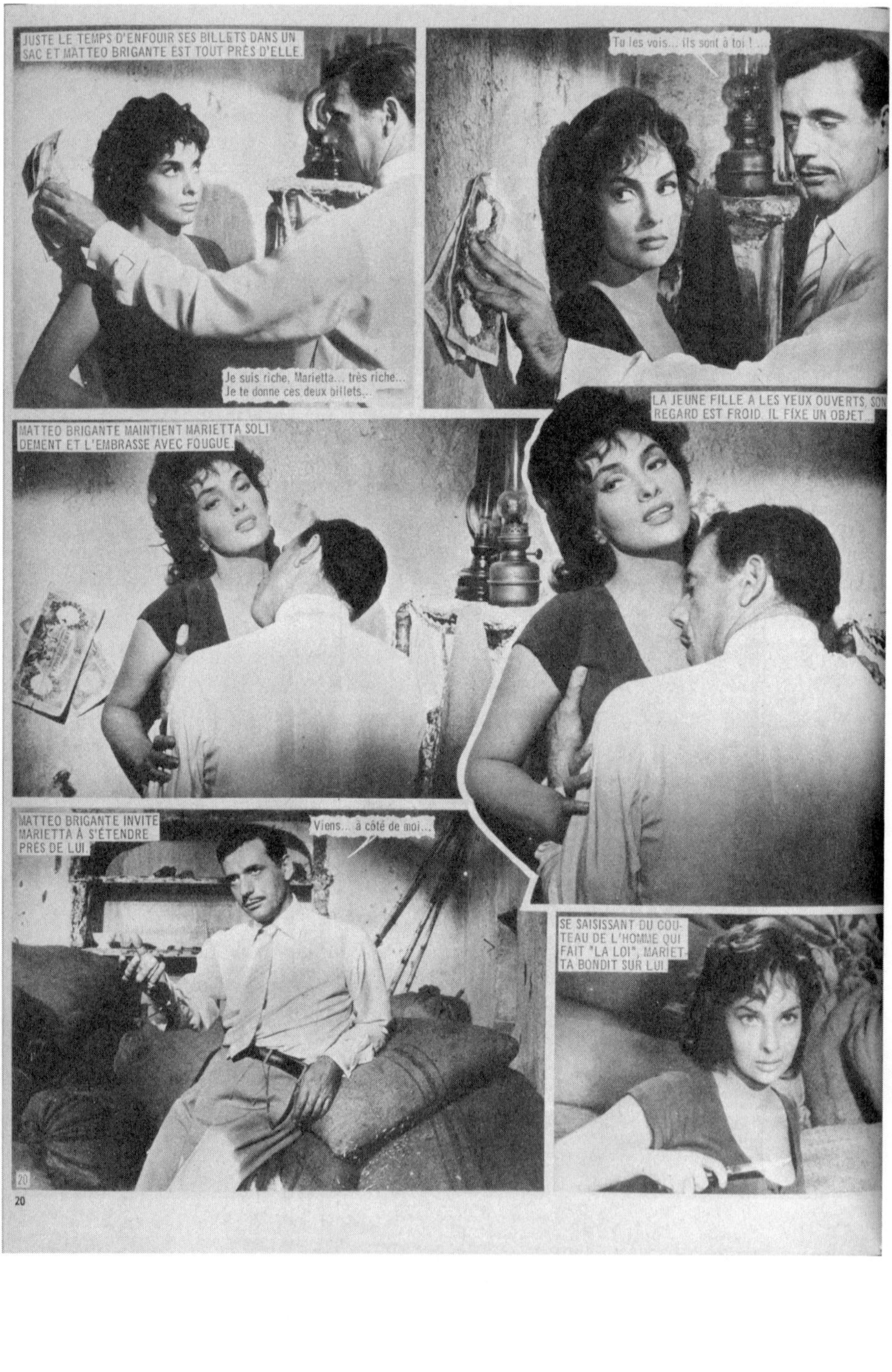

FIGURE 4.6. *"La Loi"* (La Legge, *1959, Jules Dassin),* Nous Deux Film, *July–September 1959, p. 20.*

heritage, including France's literary heritage, and to "buy" a certain form of prestige and status otherwise denied to the ideologically suspect film-photonovel and romance genres.[3] Whereas "The Law" reveals the tension between the film photonovel and celebrity culture, "The Charterhouse of Parma" exposes a similar tension between the film photonovel and the idea of national heritage. At the same time, it ties in with many aspects of celebrity culture, a feature impossible to avoid in women's magazines. The movie adapted by *Nous Deux Film* was not a recent one; thirteen years separated the release of the film and its publication as a film photonovel. And, although Christian-Jacque's film was famous in its time, its cultural position in 1961 was less assured, no longer for literary reasons—in 1948, many Stendhal fans were scandalized by what they judged to be an unfaithful adaptation that turned away from the wit and psychological depth of the novel to embrace an action-movie spirit—but for cinematographic ones: the type of cinema illustrated by the director was seen as old-fashioned.

The event that triggered the publication of the film photonovel was the death of its main actor, Gérard Philipe, a kind of French James Dean, who had died suddenly one year prior. The *Nous Deux Film* issue is one long tribute to the star, who appears on the front and the back covers of the magazine, a rather unusual move in and of itself, as well as in most of the reportage in the issue, an even more unusual decision. The film photonovel is relatively short, occupying thirty-eight of the sixty-four pages of the issue, a brief span compared with the 153-minute running time of the movie. The most plausible explanation is that the magazine wanted to save space for Philipe himself. He is less present in the film photonovel than Gina Lollobrigida is in "The Law," appearing in 74 of the 193 photos, and sometimes barely detectable. In more than one scene, Philipe is nothing but a profile in the background, and in some crowd scenes, he is hardly even recognizable. In the movie, Philipe had to share screen space with several other lead actors and actresses, and the only way to pay him a fitting tribute in the magazine was to complement the film photonovel with other material: reportage, testimonies, biography, filmography, and celebrity pictures.

In "The Law," the film photonovel was not "with" or "by" Gina Lollobrigida, but really "of" her, since nobody cared about the director, the screenwriter, or the novelist whose work had been adapted. The situation of "The Charterhouse of Parma" was totally different. The movie was based on a masterpiece of French romantic writing by an immensely popular novelist, Marie-Henri Beyle, aka Stendhal, and its director, Christian-Jacque, was a prototypical practitioner of the French "cinema of quality" school of filmmaking, the culturally and politically dominant type of cinema between 1930 and 1955, which privileged not the director but the scriptwriter and the actor. In this school, film was considered a modernized version of theater, hence the emphasis on dialogue and acting. In the poetics of the French cinema of quality, which was, in the first place, an ideology, film had a strong political agenda. The popular art of cinema, which was widely accessible at the time, had to play a key role in modern democracy and to popularize national culture, hence the focus on the adaptation of literary masterpieces and the double aspiration to remain faithful to the original and to add a contemporary political message to the film version.[5] It was this type of state-sponsored, protectionist cinema that the new generation of critics at the journal *Cahiers du cinéma* debunked and replaced with the new spirit of auteur filmmaking, which foregrounded directors and their worldview. Times had already changed by 1961, and in cinephile milieus, not much was left of the intellectual and cultural prestige of the French cinema of quality. When *Nous Deux Film* released the film-photonovel version of *The Charterhouse of Parma*, it was possible only because of the combined aura of Stendhal and Gérard Philipe.

The dichotomy between the standing of the source material (Stendhal, Philipe) and its cultural treatment (Christian-Jacque) is easily detectable in the *Nous Deux Film* version, which is torn between contradictory imperatives. First is the need to foreground a recently deceased cult actor, but what was possible with "The Law" was impossible with "The Charterhouse of Parma." There is also the cultural pressure to avoid frivolousness and gratuitous effects. Since the film photonovel is rather ill suited to reproduce "action scenes," no reader would have been surprised by the emphasis placed on portraits of the actors. The representation of the cast is clearly given priority at the expense of the plot. Many photographs are static close-ups or medium close shots of the leading actors: not only Gérard Philipe but also Maria Casarès (as the Duchess Sanseverina) and Renée Faure (as Clélia). The page layouts are relatively simple, tending to highlight the portrait, yet always in a rhetorically and narratively motivated way. The portraits are never full-page images that interrupt the story.

Take, for instance, the double spread in figure 4.7, by far the most carefully edited pages of the whole work. This clever design is an outstanding example of a well-balanced, symmetrical composition that nevertheless manages to indicate a strong psychological tension in the narrative. On top, we find four of the five protagonists of the story, not in a dull portrait gallery but in a dynamic alignment that highlights the amorous conflicts driving the plot. On the top left are the two politicians who run the city-state of Parma, the king and his prime minister—the former a dictatorial buffoon, the latter, though highly placed, a powerless puppet. On the top right are two young people who will become lovers but are meeting for the first time: Clélia, the daughter of the city prison chief, whose simplicity and honesty are expressed by her humble attitude and the high angle from which she is shot, which stresses her vulnerability, and Fabrice del Dongo, the story's hero, represented in a pose that reminds us of the official and grandiose portraits of kings and rulers, an ironic contrast to his position as a romantic outsider in the world of wealth and power. Fabrice is also the only character who looks straight into the eyes of the reader—in sharp contrast with the king, who looks away from the spectator while mimicking, like Fabrice, the hand-in-waistcoat gesture originated by Napoleon.[6] At the top of the double spread, the absence of the fifth protagonist, the Duchess Sanseverina, is as important as the presence of this symphony of looking and being seen. The duchess is the unhappy protector of the young Fabrice—she hopes to make him her lover, an offer he will refuse in spite of all of her sacrifices—and the object of a ferocious rivalry between the king, who desperately wants to seduce her, and the prime minister, her official lover. She appears in four of the next six photographs, but her "lower" place in the page layout symbolically announces her defeat, and the pictures that show her on the arm of Fabrice (the two small pictures on the right page) do not suggest a high degree of intimacy.

Spreads such as this one are exceptional in the film photonovel version of *The Charterhouse of Parma*, which adapts the movie rather limply. The famous scene in which Fabrice escapes from the city prison, for instance, which is one of the best-known and most loved scenes of nineteenth-century fiction, must have disappointed many of those who had seen the movie. In general, the layout techniques of the work are shallow, and the film photonovel struggles with the difficulty of compressing a two-and-a-half-hour movie with much witty dialogue onto a thirty-eight-page canvass. The verbal dimension is overwhelmingly present—the relative verbal brevity seen in the double spread analyzed above is not representative of the rest of the work—and the text is not that of Stendhal but the formulaic voice-over. In addition, the text frequently destroys the generally well-crafted symmetry of the visual grid while insufficiently compensating for the often elliptic treatment of several key scenes. All these problems, however, are not characteristic of this specific adaptation alone, but almost organically inherent in an approach that wants to have the best of too many worlds.

FIGURE 4.7. *"La Chartreuse de Parme" (*La Chartreuse de Parme*, 1948, Christian-Jacque),* Nous Deux Film*, April–June 1961, pp. 6–7.*

LA JOLIE CLÉLIA, LA FILLE DU GOUVERNEUR DE LA CITA-DELLE, S'INCLINE À SON TOUR DEVANT LA PRINCESSE.
FABRICE LA REGARDE. ÉMERVEILLÉ PAR TANT DE CHARME ET DE SIMPLICITÉ.
LA SANSEVERINA REJOINT FABRICE ET L'ENTRAÎNE VERS LA SORTIE DU SALON
Merci d'être venue me délivrer.
Comme je voudrais partir avec toi ... loin de tous ces fantoches ! ...
LE PRINCE N'A D'YEUX QUE POUR LA DUCHESSE. IL BRÛLE DE FAIRE D'ELLE SA MAÎTRESSE ET N'HÉSITERAIT PAS À JETER SON «AMI» MOSCA DANS UNE CELLULE DE LA CITADELLE SI LA SANSE-VERINA ACCEPTAIT ENFIN D'ÊTRE À LUI !
ERNEST IV S'ENNUIE DANS SON PALAIS. SON VISAGE N'EXPRIME QUE LA HARGNE ET LA MÉCHANCETÉ.
7

The Bozzesi Touch

A different strategy was followed by the Bozzesi publications and their French flagship magazines: the large-format *Star Ciné Roman* and the smaller *Les Films pour vous* (both published from 1956; the first Bozzesi magazines in Italy appeared somewhat earlier). The Bozzesi touch, so to speak, illustrates the law of the "handicap of the head start," which hints at the danger that conservatism may hinder initially successful decisions. This publisher was unanimously praised for his normalization of page layouts and word-and-image relationships, but the very success of this policy prevented him from considering innovations, despite the need to counterbalance the somewhat stiff and monotonous formula with smaller and larger layout surprises. The Bozzesi magazines were, thus, very efficient at solving the key issue of readability, yet weaker when it came to exploring alternatives and variations. Of all the film-photonovel magazines, the Bozzesi publications most stalwartly focused on the film photonovel, downplaying the peritext, which was given much less space. This formula blocked the use of frivolous or divergent layouts. In fact, the Bozzesi house style allowed for the insertion of large or full-page set pictures only to interrupt three-by-two grid compositions based on film stills.

We can look, for instance, at "Trapeze," the adaptation of a 1956 circus film of the same name starring Burt Lancaster, Tony Curtis, and, of course, Gina Lollobrigida. The fifty-six-page film photonovel follows the clear but rigid Bozzesi style. At regular intervals, it is interrupted, however, by larger set pictures, either full-page photographs or images occupying two-thirds of the page. Here is a list of these interruptions:

Page 4: Gina and the circus director (two-thirds)
Page 16: Gina (two-thirds)
Page 19: Gina (full)
Page 21: Gina (full)
Page 25: Gina and Burt (two-thirds)
Page 33: Gina, Burt, and Tony (two-thirds)
Page 35: Gina and Tony (full)
Page 38: Gina and Tony (full)
Page 50: Burt (full)
Page 52: Gina and Tony (full)
Page 57: Tony and Burt (two-thirds)

These eleven pictures reveal it all: the love interest of the movie; the fight between the two rivals; the success of one of them (Tony Curtis, the younger one); and, thus, the defeat of the other one (Burt Lancaster, the older one). In this discontinuous sequence of large images, only Gina Lollobrigida and Tony Curtis appear as a couple. Burt Lancaster is shown as a solitary character. And the eventual reconciliation of the two male rivals marginalizes the initial love object. The last large image, on page 57, just before the end of the story, shows the handshake between Curtis and Lancaster. But there is no longer any place for Lollobrigida, massively present in the first half. "Trapeze" tells the story of a symbolic struggle between father and son, between an old trapeze artist (initially reluctant to train his successor) and a possible competitor. But since the story is a romance, the stakes of their conflict include possession of a young woman. The whole story derives from the eleven large pictures that punctuate the film photonovel. In other words, these set pictures are a mise en abyme (image within an image) that serves multiple purposes. They compensate for the poorly printed and unusually unglamorous film stills (the overall visual quality of the film photonovel is pitiable). And they offer a welcome alternative to the larger narrative itself, which contains a lot of telling but, sadly, little showing. Granted, the plot is faithfully reproduced, and there is a lot to read, but the static film photonovel cannot compete with the spectacular shooting of the trapeze stunts. This double compensation works fairly well, for the full-page pictures are visually stimulating—they have real sex appeal and cater to various audiences—and they are so well chosen and arranged that the story within a story becomes the perfect substitute for an otherwise heavily told and verbally overcrowded narrative.

Another innovation of the Bozzesi magazines raises a fascinating theoretical question, that of the quasi absence of a type of grid that might have seemed natural to use in the years of triumphant wide-screen movies, but that is almost never found in the film photonovel: the three-by-one grid, that is, a page layout based on three wide images replicating the panoramic features of the projection on screen.

The adaptation of *Helen of Troy*, a 1956 Italo-American peplum shot in Cinecittà and starring Rossana Podestà (one of the countless competitors of Gina Lollobrigida and Sophia Loren in the mid-1950s), was the perfect film photonovel response to the success of wide-screen cinema after 1953, when this formerly common technique reappeared in Hollywood in order to combat the fall in attendance due, in part, to the emergence of television. The *Star Ciné Roman* adaptation of this Robert Wise movie runs to sixty pages, and more than a third of them have a three-by-one page layout (see fig. 4.8). A comparable number have a two-tier structure, either a page divided into two comparable single-image tiers (six pages appear to follow this model) or a page divided in two tiers with one large and two smaller images (eleven pages). Full-page images are relative rare (four pages), and

FIGURE 4.8. *"Hélène de Troie" (*Helen of Troy*, 1956, Robert Wise),* Star Ciné Roman, *1 July 1958, p. 13.*

the remaining spreads introduce tiny variations on the two- or three-tier layout type.

"Helen of Troy" is a well-made and efficient example (easy to read and visually impressive) of how the film photonovel could offer a plausible print version of a peplum melodrama. The question is therefore not what makes the three-by-one formula strong but what makes it rare. For despite the commercial ascendancy of wide-screen technology, single-image-tier layouts never found great success in the film-photonovel business, as can be seen in the use of traditional three-by-two models in comparable movie adaptations, such as *Samson and Delilah* (Cecil B. DeMille, 1949), *The Silver Chalice* (Victor Saville, 1954), *Ulysses* (Mario Camerini, 1954), and *Solomon and Sheba* (King Vidor, 1959), among others, which rely partially on large single-image tiers. The example of *Helen of Troy* shows that the formula works only when certain conditions are met. Among them, two are chief: first, it is necessary that the plot be utterly simple. To smoothly tell a story with only three images per page—and not too much text, either within the image panel or in separate text panels, which would hinder the visual pleasure of the remarkable photographs—the story must avoid any form of narrative complexity. It is useless to say that the reinterpretation of the myth of Helen of Troy is a fitting example of such an elementary plot. One does not have to know Homer's epic and its larger story world to fully enjoy the Hollywood reinterpretation, which is reductive but extremely powerful (featuring betrayal, jealousy, and vengeance, along with the classic cocktail of sex appeal and misogyny). Second, it should be possible to combine the three-by-one grid with star or celebrity photography so that the insertion of close-ups and portraits does not disrupt the overall tone of the work.

In "Helen of Troy," this is achieved, for instance, by the multiplication of so-called two shots, which replace the traditional shot-reverse-shot technique and provide a visual take that is highly attractive in a large-screen format. Two faces or two characters fill an ultralarge screen much better than just one face or one character. The panoramic tiers and the combination of two- and three-tier layouts also guarantee a fluid transition from multiple-image spreads to full-image pages. The latter are no longer experienced as alien elements interfering with the story—a problem that characterizes many film-still adaptations that try to enhance their visual quality by including some larger set pictures. "Trapeze" showed that large and full-page images, when cleverly selected and arranged, can retell the story in a different mode. But not all film photonovels succeed in doing so, and there often remains a gap between intertwined film stills and set pictures.

Not all movies allow for such a treatment, and even in "Helen of Troy," the reader may find the three-by-one or two-by-one page layouts a little dull and flat. That is probably the reason why the work progressively introduces tiny variations on the basic scheme, sometimes in somewhat gratuitous ways that betray an affected endeavor to make changes for the sake of changes.

The most important lesson that one can draw from "Helen of Troy" is twofold. It demonstrates the difficulty of fully embracing a page layout that radically diverges from the genre norm, which supposes the fragmentation of each tier by at least two images. Sequentiality seems harder to achieve if tiers contain no more than one image, as if the supremacy of the horizontal lines was experienced as something that jeopardized both linearity and narrativity, bringing the narrative to a kind of standstill while preventing the page from offering narratively attractive sequences. The basic anxiety inspired by the three-by-one page layout can be explained by a paradoxical form of iconophobia: in a film photonovel, the deployment of too few images on a page foregrounds visuality in too exaggerated a way and, thus, endangers both the instrumental use of images in the unfolding of the narrative and their mere use as a device of storytelling.

Moreover, and this is a second conclusion to draw, the page layout of "Helen of Troy" makes clear how much the basic unit of the film photonovel is the page. In "Helen of Troy," the three-tier structure allows for stunning visual compositions, but at the risk of slowing down the plot. Their strength, when carefully executed, is to upgrade the sequentially organized pictures in aesthetically satisfying configurations, harmoniously superposed onto the grid and never intruding on the readability of images or story. The most salient techniques are the chiasm, or mirror effect, and the abstract geometrical shapes, most of them triangular, that emerge in an overview of all of the pictures on the page. Certain double spreads exemplify both these figures.

Film photonovels with more images per page have fewer chances to produce these kinds of meta-images, which almost appear as watermarks under the linear surface of the photographs. This does not mean, however, that they cannot produce special page effects of their own, as demonstrated, for example, by the divergent-corner technique examined earlier.

Down and Dirty? The Case of *Amor Film*

Much has been said about *Amor Film*, the magazine that most film-photonovel fans love to hate. *Amor Film*, which published film photonovels between 1957 and 1963, was a longtime competitor of magazines such as

Mon Film, and specialized in short illustrated novelizations, along with a great deal of movie gossip. Its selection of films for adaptation was not completely different from what others were doing, mixing several genres and both lesser- and better-known productions.[7] Also, *Amor Film*'s reliance exclusively on set pictures was not a differentiating feature; *Mon Film*, which was often praised as a straightforward and refreshing magazine, also used them. What does differentiate one from the other is the widely shared impression that the *Amor Film* adaptations are "unreadable," being both difficult to follow and unpleasant to experience. One can easily understand the source of this impression. The magazine's stories are short (sometimes less than twenty pages long); they have no more than three or four pictures per page; they are littered with large heaps of text, which do not necessarily match any visual counterpart; their pace is irregular and full of gaps and narrative jump cuts; and last but not least, they use a page layout that is disruptive to the viewer, to put it mildly: tier-size images obliquely arranged and always overlapping, as if a three-story building were collapsing after a violent earthquake (see fig. 4.9).

At first sight, the layout in figure 4.9 stands out as a one-off in the history of film photonovels. It is also the only example that credits its typographer: a certain R. Gendre (possibly a pseudonym). That *Amor Film* was published by a small provincial company, Les Éditions du Rempart in Lyon (which specialized in comics), is not enough to explain its bizarre layout. To understand why *Amor Film* was different from other film-photonovel venues, one has to look at the magazine itself. *Amor Film* was the first instance of a movie magazine—dedicated to a mix of gossip, reportage, and illustrated mini-novelizations—turning into a film-photonovel magazine. These short novelizations, almost as old as cinema itself, retell, in short-story format (usually a few pages), the content of a movie in a formulaic, reader's-digest-like style. Generally, they are heavily illustrated with large star-oriented set pictures. The formula is not necessarily lowbrow; it is also typical of middlebrow publications such as *Life*, although not with the same wildly expressive layout is seen in *Amor Film*. Each issue of the latter combines one film photonovel with a number of other sections: a gossip column, correspondence requests, movie news, and a selection of short novelizations. The 1 July 1962 issue, for instance, boasts an extension of the page count to fifty-two (perhaps to compensate for a recent increase in the sales price; this figure includes the four cover pages). It has the following table of contents:

Front cover: pinup picture of Dany Saval, a former rival of Brigitte Bardot, who is announced as the star of the film photonovel of the

FIGURE 4.9. *"L'Enquête mystérieuse" (*The Frightened City*, 1961, John Lemont),* Amor Film*, 1 July 1962, n.p. [6].*

month. This appears to be a hoax, however, for Saval merely plays a part in one of the other movies that are discussed elsewhere in the issue, not in the film photonovel. This page is the only one that is in full color. All other pages are black-and-white, including the back cover, which clearly signifies a "cheap" publication.

Interior front cover: a risqué full-page snapshot illustrating the shooting of a 1962 sketch film, *The Seven Deadly Sins.*

Page 1: some short editorial announcements and a large picture of Anita Ekberg, famously known for the Trevi Fountain scene in Fellini's *La Dolce Vita*; the caption identifies her as one of the actresses in another sketch film with multiple directors, *Boccaccio 70* (1962).

Pages 2–19: film-photonovel version of the gangster movie *The Frightened City* (John Lemont, 1961), a British neo-noir produced by Allied Artists and costarring Sean Connery.

Pages 20–21: a double spread with brief-captioned pictures of celebrities.

Page 22: a brief but heavily illustrated editorial note on two films that impressed audiences at the recent Cannes Film Festival, *The Lovers of Teruel* (*Les Amants de Teruel*, Raymond Rouleau, 1962) and *Boccaccio 70.*

Pages 23–27: an illustrated novelization of *The Lovers of Teruel*, with a text panel about its lead actress, Ludmila Tchérina.

Pages 28–32: an illustrated novelization of the Fellini sketch, featuring Anita Ekberg, in *Boccaccio 70.*

Page 33: a pinup photo of Romy Schneider, another actress starring in *Boccaccio 70.*

Page 34: a presentation of Julien Duvivier's *The Devil and the Ten Commandments* (*Le Diable et les dix commandements*), also from 1962, followed by a mini-novelization of one of its ten sketches.

Pages 35–37: a heavily illustrated interview with Jean-Luc Godard about the shooting of *My Life to Live* (*Vivre sa vie*, released later in 1962).

Pages 38–39: an illustrated interview with the makers of *Tartarin of Tarascon* (*Tartarin de Tarascon* (Francis Blanche, 1962), based on a story by the then popular, "typically French" nineteenth-century writer Alphonse Daudet.

Pages 40–41: a heavily illustrated mini-novelization of Pietro Germi's *Divorce Italian Style* (1961), with a brief interview with the director.

Page 42: illustrations of a jazz band, probably the band that plays in *La Parisienne* (Michel Boisrond, 1957), a Brigitte Bardot movie.
Page 43: a pinup photo of Virna Lisi, who appears in *Romulus and Remus*, a 1961 peplum directed by Sergio Corbucci.
Pages 44–45: gossip section.
Pages 46–48: correspondence-request section.
Interior back cover: a pinup photo of Micheline Presle.
Back cover: a second pinup photo of Dany Saval, now captioned as starring in *The Seven Deadly Sins* (see the front cover).

Amor Film was a magazine in which no square millimeter was without print. Putting aside the film-photonovel section, the images, which occupy at least 80 percent of the available space, are printed with no margins. The overall impression is of a magazine that works to overpower the reader, a male-targeted audience. The celebrity photography turns into pinup photography. The focus on "quality" movies systematically strays into scandalous themes, sexual in nature (the theme of the Godard movie is prostitution, for instance), and the "dynamic" page layout differs from what other, more romance-oriented magazines offered. There are good reasons to ask whether *Amor Film*, which never diverted from its house style, is part of the film-photonovel genre. The case can be made that in its form, it is. From other perspectives, the production does not entirely fit with the genre.

A reading of the magazine clarifies what happens in the film photonovel. As mentioned, *Amor Film* did not adopt a format that dropped the tradition of the photonovel in favor of that of the film photonovel—though this was the procedure of many magazines before they returned, in the mid-1960s, to the photonovel environment. *Amor Film* transferred the essential features of the illustrated novelization to the domain of the film photonovel without forsaking its origins. The magazine's adaptations are illustrated novelizations disguised as film photonovels, as a comparison between a work such as "The Frightened City" (from the first half of the issue under consideration) and the mini-novelizations in the second half makes clear. The selection of the images (sensational pictures rather than ones that help tell the story), the layout principles privileging a shocking montage of overlapping photographs, jagged edges, erratically inserted text panels (rather than speech balloons or captions), and a systematic but rapidly wearing effort to "make it new" are elements copied from the expressive typography of the reportage and short novelizations in the second part of the magazine. Even the countless technical mistakes can be accounted for from this perspective. In many panels in *Amor Film*, the reading order is fundamentally disrupted, and one finds dialogue in which the answer (on the left) precedes the question (on the right) or in which it is almost impossible to guess the correct way to move from text to image and vice versa. All these errors dissolve in a reading regime that does not consider the verbal and the visual elements to be alternating parts of the same narrative string, but rather the result of a collage of strings of texts and images brutally glued together in different schemes. If one has to read the text from A to Z in order to grasp the sense of the story, one can browse the images in any order without losing any essential information.

Amor Film is, therefore, a symptom of the continuing pressure exerted by larger media networks, popular movie magazines in this case, that never ceased to surround the film photonovel as a cultural industry. Niche publications such as the film photonovel could not exist without the larger context of a wide range of narrated cinema publications and, more generally, models of words and images interacting in the field of mass-media magazines. While *Amor Film* may have engendered a totally unreadable type of film photonovel, it nonetheless helped reveal part of the hidden logic of the medium. For that reason, it would be a mistake not to consider it a historically central publication.

5 / Action? Stop! Pose and Movement

Despite the numerous, radical transformations in the global framing of the narrative in film photonovels—as shown by the systematic addition of a voice-over and the pressure to turn many works into melodramas—the genre proved capable of reproducing the plot and story world of a movie. Most adaptations smoothly replicate the basic events, characters, motivations, settings, and even rhythms of their original. It would be inaccurate to assume that film photonovels give a less faithful representation of a film than, for instance, a published script or an authorized novelization. Yet at least one aspect seemed to resist the transfer from one sign system to another. How can fixed images, whether set pictures or film stills, compete with the dynamic character of a projected movie? At a purely theoretical level, it is easy to deconstruct the difference between the fixed and the mobile (Hoelzl and Marie 2015). In practice, however, the shift from film to photo magazine was not a minor operation, and since the ambition of the film photonovel was neither to extract from the original movie a set of independently functioning glamour pictures nor to simply document the "making of" the movie, an in-depth reflection on the creative tension between fixed and mobile images is a must for any study of the genre.

Pregnant or Indecisive Moments?

The basic question is this: does every picture tell a story? The answer is yes—or rather, some pictures do or at least can do so. The classic example is still the "pregnant image" as theorized by G. E. Lessing, a concept central to the debate on time and the fixed image. A "pregnant moment" image is a subtype of the more general category of "decisive moment" pictures, best illustrated by the work of photojournalists such as Henri Cartier-Bresson, and it is generally defined as a type of picture that allows the viewer to deduce from the selected moment of an action what happened before and what is about to happen.

A second type of image appears to host the same narrative impulses, those studied by Victor Burgin in his landmark publication *The Remembered Film* (Burgin 2004, 23–28). Certain movie images, Burgin argues, are situated between an "image," that is, a fixed and single image, and an "image sequence," that is, a succession of related images telling an event or a story. They are what he calls "sequence-images," or images exceeding the disjunction of fixed and mobile, isolated and continuous, and they may occur in several ways. For instance, when remembered by the spectator, they are capable of triggering a narrative reconstruction of a whole story, thanks to the emotional force that accompanies them, which may or may not coincide with what was seen on screen.

As demonstrated by Lessing and Burgin, pictures can tell stories via the interaction between two elements: the intrinsic properties of the images (not every painting represents a pregnant moment, not every movie image can become the support of a process of remembrance and reinvention) and the cognitive hardware and software of reader and spectator, who can activate mental actions, schemes, and frames as well as personal memories to transform a single fixed image into a visual narrative stream.

The narrative reading of a fixed image goes beyond the injection of a temporal layer into the image, a sign long considered purely spatial, that is, open to immediate, nontemporal understanding. It is now common knowledge that looking at pictures is a temporal phenomenon as well. It takes time to see what seems to be offered in a single timeless glance. The narrative reading of a fixed image is also more complex than the purely subjective and aleatory projection of a time span onto the image's surface. That said, reading a film photonovel cannot be reduced to narrative deciphering of its images. Such a procedure reduces the film photonovel to the materiality of its individual photographic components or building blocks without taking into account that the basic unit of the genre is the page, specifically, pages of sequentially arranged photographs meant to be read in a given order: one image after another, one page after another.

The consequences of this sequential simultaneity, or simultaneous sequentiality, can be observed at all levels, including, for instance, images of the type used in nearly all film photonovels. Although the genre tries to give an idea of the general story line of a film, hardly any attempt is made to prioritize images that suggest or reproduce action and movement at more than a local, anecdotal level. The deletion of images detailing the spatial context of the action—landscapes, for instance—has been underlined time and again by those writing on the film photonovel, but the erasure of culminating action scenes is no less striking. Some far-reaching stylistic preferences of the film photonovel can be explained by this a priori turning away from action pictures or pictures attempting to give a sense of speed and movement (blurred images, for instance, are exceptionally rare).

First, one finds a striking absence of pregnant-moment images in the film photonovel, both among individual images and in overall page composition. Cliffhangers are rare. Small film-photonovel images are generally banal, appealing but little to the reader's narrative imagination, and turning the pages is seldom motivated mainly by the desire to see what will happen next. As the example of the *Rear Window* adaptation will demonstrate, suspense building in a film photonovel is not achieved in the same fashion as in a movie, which sticks to carefully elaborated temporal montage rules. Narratively, film-photonovel pictures may seem frustratingly shallow and banal. This banality discloses, however, a perfect understanding of the genre's medium specificity.

Second, film-photonovel images are often posed images. The reason for this is simple. Many works rely heavily on set pictures, which are always *tableau vivant*–like posed pictures, even those meant to summarize or symbolize an action shot or scene. This practice does not justify similar choices when film stills are used. But the same focus on pose and immobility is observable even in photos selected from typical action scenes. Moreover, the avoidance of action affects both the micro and macro levels of the story. Individual images are not suited to the representation of rapid action, and the complete string of images in the work often summarizes climactic moments or scenes with text panels or characters' speech. Fans of *Samson and Delilah* (1949) might be disappointed at seeing the final collapse of the temple reduced to just one small panel in the film-photonovel adaptation, but such a flattening of narrative peaks is more the rule than the exception.

A third mechanism used to downsize action and movement is the frequent repetition of comparable images, which do not appear as successive moments of an unfolding action but rather as a number of different views of the actors—more precisely, of their bodies and faces. Often, film-photonovel pages bring back the same building blocks, close-ups or two shots of the protagonists, to lay out a series of variations on faces and bodies, generally in symmetrical and foreseeable ways. These detemporalized sequences tend to replace the action, which is conveyed by the textual layers of the work. The influence of the photonovel was undoubtedly a key factor in this particular treatment of action and pose, very different from what is found in the adapted movies. What applies to the photonovel applies to the film photonovel as well. As I noted in an earlier study of the photonovel (Baetens 2013), the aesthetics of overstatement shifts focus from the classic locus of the tableau to the portrait. It is a mistake to believe that the visual string of a photonovel shows the successive parts of an action unfolding in time (as if the photonovel were offering a selection of shots from a virtual movie sequence). The visual logic of the photonovel is less syntagmatic than paradigmatic (less narrative than illustrative): it is organized around a series of variations on the face. Even if photonovels tell stories, their first concern is the portrayal of the characters.

The film photonovel does more than just reproduce the original in a different format. It goes even further by providing a genre-specific take on a movie, despite the minimalist nature of the images and page compositions—as if the film photonovel were stressing its difference from the overstatement found in the photonovel, and thereby defining its own medium specificity. This minimalism is subtle, perhaps because the narratives in film photonovels are less elaborate than the screenplays that they adapt (the issue of reduction and simplification is a recurrent complaint). This possible tension between a movie's complexity and the film photonovel's simplicity creates a need to introduce more variation at the level of the image and the page layout, the latter having more room than the former for small, "decorative" interventions.

It is crucial to stress another difference between photonovels and film photonovels: actors in the former often rivaled those in the latter in attractiveness, seductiveness, and sex appeal, but most of the time they did not reach star status in these arenas. Photonovel actors were either beginning starlets who worked in the business while waiting for their big break in the movies or aging actors who did not make it in cinema and had no choice but to specialize in less prestigious photonovel parts. The photonovel had its own big stars (for excellent work on this aspect, see Faber, Minuit and Takodjerad 2013), but they were normally not known outside the small world of that genre. In film photonovels, on the contrary, all actors are celebrities, and magazines actively used their images to promote celebrity culture and pinup photography. The reader of a film photonovel did not experience the repetition of the faces and bodies of well-known actors as something harmful. Since these faces and bodies were judged to be admirable and sexy, even perfect, their endless repetition, as seen, for instance, in the case of Gina Lollobrigida in "The Law," could only contribute to the aura of an actor or an actress, and serve as a corollary to the pleasure of the reader, who was often more interested in the star than in the story.

There are other reasons why the opposition between fixed and mobile images no longer holds in the century-old debate about the single image. Chief among them is the presence of textual accompaniment in the film photonovel, which temporalizes the photograph in two ways. First, it projects a temporal span onto the visual simultaneity of the picture—one can have a snapshot image of two characters talking to each other, but the time it would take for them to pronounce the words printed in the speech balloons exceeds the brief moment of the picture. Second, text elongates reading time and pace—just having to read the words one after another jeopardizes the illusion of timelessness in the picture.

Things change even more radically when one takes into account the shift from single images to sequential images. The film photonovel is never a single-panel story in the style of a single-panel comic (such as *Dennis the Menace*). Pages that contain only one image are part of a larger sequence, which they can interrupt but never completely supersede. The sequential arrangement automatically translates into a temporalized narrative reading. Even very similar images are read one after another and are thus cognitively converted into a temporal and perhaps even intensely narrativized string. A succession of similar images is "naturally" understood as representing the transition of a character or an object through several moments in time. The global narrative framework of the film-photonovel genre lends emphasis to this way of reading. In spite of the film photonovel's tendency toward repetition, its narrative drive is, therefore, never in danger.

Stasis and Movement on the Page

It is not enough to underline the intertwined simultaneity and consecutiveness, as well as the combined use of static and repeated images, in a genre that can retell a movie's story without strong visual sequentiality. One has to understand which mechanisms organize the tension between time and space when it comes to selecting or editing images on the page. The fundamental editing principle of the film photonovel is the shift from temporal to spatial montage. Since the story is mainly told by the verbal components, the visual part of the work can be used for different purposes.

A superficial glance might make it seem as if the images were purely illustrative, that is, narratively redundant. In this view, what is shown simply repeats what is being said or told, and this illustrative function renders the images fundamentally superfluous. And while it is possible to read and fully understand most film photonovels without ever looking at the pictures, this is not what happens. For the role of the images is not only to reinforce the text, but also to compose figures of their own, purely visual figures that add a nonverbal, nonnarrative layer to the whole work.

All film photonovel readers are immediately struck by two features of the genre: the scarcity of action pictures and action sequences, and the ubiquity of wallpaper pages, that is, pages containing similar images of figures in similar positions (see fig. 5.1). The overall visual impression is that of the endless reappearance of a wallpaper motif. Like the three-by-two grid, the static wallpaper structure seems to be part of the genre's DNA.

Like this type of grid, the wallpaper composition is the starting point for countless simple but incredibly efficient (both economically and visually attractive) variations. Each of them introduces a minimum of real diversity in the underlying model, which is forcefully strengthened by the multiple reuses it allows for. We have already presented the divergent-corner technique, based on the nonrepetition of a motif in the upper-left or lower-right corners of the classic grid. There are at least two more variations: the checkerboard structure, which complicates the wallpaper motif by crossing or alternating two motifs, each row being a chiasmic echo of the preceding and following ones; and the diagonal structure, which divides the page into two complementary triangular wallpaper structures. With minimal changes, it becomes possible to produce infinite aesthetically pleasant variations on these basic types, as seen, for instance, in figure 5.2.

Compositions like these produce a spatial movement that is typical of (although not exclusive to) the film photonovel. These layouts always take the page—or in some cases, the double page—as their fundamental unit. Grids and wallpapers may cover the whole work, but the specific way in which they do so generally changes page after page. Each page tells an autonomous part of the story (Baetens 2015), and once the reader is familiar with this particular editing technique, there is no need to hide, with the help of continuity editing, or to exaggerate, with the help of cliffhangers and other suspense devices, the transition from one page to another. What happens instead is the activation of a visual solidarity between left and right pages. A kind of "metagrid" appears, engendering reading patterns that transgress the autonomy and internal hierarchy of the single page. This phenomenon expands on the aforementioned reshaping of page layouts and reading trajectories according to vertical columns

FIGURE 5.1. *"Monte-Carlo" (*The Monte Carlo Story*, 1957, Sam Taylor/Giulio Macchi),* Ciné Succès*, July 1962, p. 38.*

FIGURE 5.2. *"Les Voies du Cœur"* (Le vie del cuore, *1942, Camillo Mastrocinque),* Ciné Succès, *August 1961, p. 31.*

instead of horizontal rows. In the film photonovel, the transgression of the classic distinction between left and right pages, and of the reading order it involves, is not realized through the production of double-spread images—a technique well known in comic books—but through the power of visual lines and orientations that challenge the internal structure of the autonomous page.

Let's Dance

As mentioned, the film photonovel tends to delete or downsize action scenes, even those representing turning points in the story. The mythic final shootout of most westerns, for instance, often detailed according to genre conventions, is, in its film photonovel version, generally reduced to a single panel, sometimes more hinted at than punctiliously described. A typical example of such a shortening is found in the adaptation of *Johnny Guitar* (Nicholas Ray, 1954), which simplifies the ultimate duel to next to nothing, to the extent of wiping out the role of the character who fires the decisive shot. What is suggested by the film-photonovel version (*Star Ciné Roman*, 1960) is, indeed, something other than what happens in the movie. In the latter, Emma (the "bad" character) is shot by the strong-willed saloonkeeper, Vienna (the "good" character), the rivalry between the two resulting from, among other things, their having been rivals in love. In the film photonovel, readers unfamiliar with the plot of the film might be under the assumption that Emma is killed not by Vienna but by Vienna's former (and also current) lover, the man called Johnny Guitar. The reason for this curious twist might be ideological: not because it reestablishes the clear-cut dichotomy between good and evil (Johnny is no less complex a character than Vienna), but because it patriarchally relocates the use of "acceptable" violence to the male character. The film clearly sides with Johnny and Vienna, presenting Emma as a morally despicable person. The difference between the ending of the movie and that of the film photonovel is, however, no less a consequence of the strong preference of the adapting genre than of static representations.

An interesting case in this regard is the treatment of dance scenes. A typical example of action and movement, they are also a chief ingredient of melodrama. As convincingly argued by Richard Dyer (1992) in his study of the often despised Hollywood musical, dance scenes do not interrupt narrative scenes in order to offer escapist relief from harsher and more realistic plot elements. Instead, they propose a utopian alternative that should be read politically.

In the treatment of dance scenes, the film photonovel is caught between two contradictory imperatives. On the one hand, the genre has to limit the place of dance scenes, which "naturally" resist being frozen in posed pictures. On the other hand, the film photonovel must emphasize their role in order to foster a melodramatic interpretation of the whole work. The deletion of dance scenes is, therefore, more than the symptom of a technical problem: it is the index of an ideological reframing. In *Pane, amore e . . .* (*Scandal in Sorrento*, 1955), the third entry in the *Bread and Love* series, there is an exemplary dance scene in which Vittorio De Sica, who plays the marshal in all three films,[1] and Sophia Loren (Donna Sofia, his love interest in this film) execute a funny mambo. The scene is pivotal to the story: it provokes both the final separation of the lovers and Donna Sofia's eventual choice of the poor fisherman Nicolino, her real love. The first (French) film-photonovel version of the movie, in the prestigious large-size *Star Ciné Roman* (no. 107, 15 March 1961), could have easily kept this long and hilarious sequence: it highlights the beauty and wit of Sophia Loren, and it focuses on the love triangle. But the dance scene did not make it into the film photonovel, because the adaptation clearly stresses the comedic dimension of the movie, not the melodramatic aspect, which progressively shrank throughout the three installments of this masterpiece of pink neorealism. Despite being a comedy, *Pane, Amore e Fantasia* (*Bread, Love and Dreams*, 1953) is heavily marked by melodrama and neorealism—not an unusual combination (Morreale 2011). The second film, *Pane, amore e gelosia* (US title: *Frisky*, 1954), is more of a comedy than its predecessor, hence the adjective "pink." It contains some wild dance scenes, which the film photonovel includes in a radically reduced fashion. The third film is fully an Italian comedy, stripped of its neorealist melodramatic subtext. Too strong an emphasis on the dance scene of this film would have signified a possible return to melodrama, which had ceased to be the dominant tone of the series.

There exists, however, a second adaptation of the same film, in the less prestigious *Ciné Sélection* series (no. 75, September 1962). Here the mambo scene occupies a double spread (two pages out of fifty-one; see fig. 5.3). This scene captures well the clash between stiffness and overacting: Sofia's official partner, the marshal, does not know anything about modern dance styles and hardly knows how to behave; Sofia's young worshipper, Nicolino, sulks because he misunderstands Sofia's actions; and Sofia exaggerates her body language in a final attempt to seduce Nicolino and end her engagement to the marshal. Yet the dance scene is, perhaps, not the central feature of the double spread. The prominent voice-over comments not only on what happens but also, in great detail, on what is in the minds of all three characters; in this regard, the showing of the dance

FIGURE 5.3. *"Pain, amour et . . ." (*Pane, amore e . . . *, 1955, Dino Risi),* Ciné Sélection, *September 1962, pp. 48–49.*

...LE PAUVRE DON ANTONIO FAIT DE GRANDS EFFORTS POUR SUIVRE, SANS CEPENDANT Y PARVENIR, LES ÉTRANGES VIREVOLTES DE LA JEUNE FEMME. DE TOUTE ÉVIDENCE, IL NE CONNAÎT PAS TRÈS BIEN LES DANSES MODERNES, ET IL FAIT CE QU'IL PEUT...
APRÈS LE MAMBO, C'EST ERIKA QUI VEUT DANSER AVEC LE COMMANDANT. MAIS DÈS QUE SOFIA EST SEULE, NICOLINO VIENT S'ASSEOIR À SA TABLE.
Je viens te dire au revoir. J'ai un contrat pour le Venezuela, et je m'embarque demain.
Bon voyage!
CEPENDANT, SOFIA EST BOULEVERSÉE PAR CETTE NOUVELLE. SON COEUR EST TRISTE. TOUT À COUP, AU MOMENT OÙ ELLE ARRIVE À LA SORTIE, LE COMMANDANT LA REJOINT.
Je vais chez moi... la musique... Je suis fatiguée et triste, c'est peut-être parce que demain, il y aura juste un an que mon pauvre Pasqualino est mort...
Paix à son âme! Partons donc, je vous accompagne.
Non, non... Restez donc vous amuser... Quand je suis comme ça, il vaut mieux que je sois seule! Je suis nerveuse, don Antonio, excusez-moi! Bonsoir...

is marginalized by the telling of it. On the other hand, this double page is the only example in the whole work of a panel with a vertical layout, which shows Sofia dancing in a frame that isolates her from the rest of the scene. The mambo dance, in other words, shifts to something that all film photonovel lovers know well: the move from dialogue and action to posed pictures highlighting the male or female star.

Film photonovels with dance scenes include them in ways that combine dance and pose, time and space, as well as movement and immobility. They avoid pictures that foreground hectic or dizzying movement, taking great care to integrate the representation of the dancers in well-balanced, symmetrical page layouts. This can be seen in figure 5.4, a page from "La Princesse de Clèves." The source film (directed by Jean Delannoy, 1961, based on a script by Jean Cocteau) is another typical example of a French "cinema of quality" adaptation of a classic French novel.

A closer look at a legendary dance scene will elucidate some of the concrete technical inventions of the film photonovel intended to both include and control the potentially dangerous action scenes of bodies in motion. *Solomon and Sheba* (King Vidor, 1959) contains a gorgeous example of "cheesecake," that is, glamour photography emphasizing women's sex appeal. It is the scene in which Sheba—Gina Lollobrigida (who else?)—celebrates the rite of the pagan god Ragon before seducing King Solomon, who is about to betray his people and their God by falling into the arms of the foreign queen. In a typically eclectic Hollywood style, this stunning scene mixes a broad range of models and stimuli: American ingredients such as the Broadway ballet and musical influences; exoticizing fare such as the oriental music, which includes a stereotypical wild and heavy "primitive African" beat; choreography that is as much African as American; and a pagan idol that serves as a kind of totem around which women and warriors are screaming, shouting, and mating. In the seduction scene, there are classic allusions to Arab belly dancing and Salome's dance of veils, along with contemporary references to the then-popular Spanish corrida films—Gina Lollobrigida swinging her cape in the same way that the torero defies the raging bull, and so on.

The film-photonovel version, published in the Bozzesi flagship series *Star Ciné Roman*, devotes seven pages, an exceptional amount, to the scene. The narrative arc starts with Sheba entering the temple on a throne carried by her many followers, and finishes, after the orgy and seduction scene, with the divine punishment by Yahweh, whose thunder and lightning destroy the statue of Ragon and bring death to many present at the ceremony—including innocent victims, whose deaths will trigger King Solomon's atonement. The film photonovel reproduces the frenzy of this

FIGURE 5.4. *"La Princesse de Clèves" (*La Princesse de Clèves*, 1961, Jean Delannoy),* Nous Deux Film*, April–June 1961, p. 6.*

dance scene, which degenerates into an orgy, shown as graphically as the Hays Code allowed, but it does so in a way that succeeds in keeping wild action and movement under control and in balance with aspects of immobility and frozen imagery.

Three strategies come to the fore. First, the adaptation creates an alternate montage sequence, which includes a flashback showing a discussion between Solomon and the "good" female character of the story, the Israeli Abishag. At the end of the scene, Abishag's death provokes Solomon's first step toward repentance. The film photonovel cuts back and forth between Sheba's dance and static shots of Solomon being implored to not surrender to the queen and to not betray his people by worshipping an idol. The dialogue between Solomon and Abishag occupies a full page, which breaks the tension built up in the opening page of the scene by an establishing shot that zooms in on Sheba entering and taking off most of her clothes before starting to dance. Second, images in temporally organized sequences are arranged to mimic the explosion of bodily energy during the dance and orgy, and these are combined with large set pictures showing the seductive but posed Gina Lollobrigida. Both the picture covering two-thirds of the third page of the scene (between a full shot and a medium shot) and the full-page medium-shot picture (between a medium shot and a close-up) on page 7 interrupt the narrative continuity of the scene and alter the reading pace. Finally, long captions are added to a scene that in the movie contains only music, noise, screams, and laughter. Sheba does not have to speak to mesmerize Solomon, and the latter does not say a single word when re-undressing and kissing her ("re-undressing," since after her first undressing, and in order to redo the same semi-striptease, Sheba had put on her veil again). These captions, traditionally placed on top of the panels and easy to read, as in all Bozzesi productions, contribute to a dramatic slowing of the action.

Movement and immobility in addition to action and pose are, thus, harmoniously yet powerfully reconciled in this scene. This merger helps introduce a new question and a new challenge to the discussion on the representation of temporal progression in the film photonovel: What about narrative tension? How can one create and maintain suspense in a context of simultaneous sequentiality?

Another Form of Suspense

The thorough spatialization of action and movement and the paradoxical creation of new forms of visual mobility based on nontemporal layout principles are a great challenge to all film photonovels that adapt thrillers and action-based movies. The problem of transferring suspense from screen to page is illustrated in an example borrowed from "Volupté," the 1963 adaptation of *Go Naked in the World* (Ranald MacDougall, 1961; fig. 5.5). The character that we see performing as an amateur equilibrist is a real daredevil, but the action and subsequent suspense that are breathtaking in the film are almost completely vitiated in the film-photonovel version, in which the reader immediately notices the happy ending to the character's life-threatening acrobatics. To solve the problem of how to maintain suspense when the very page layout seems to prevent it, the maker of the film photonovel could try the cliffhanger technique. In the film photonovel, however, this is not a realistic option. First, there are not always enough pages available to lay out all the suspense elements on a page ending with such a cliffhanger. In addition, the impact of the cliffhanger technique would prove meager in a genre that swapped installment publication for

FIGURE 5.5. *"Volupté" (*Go Naked in the World*, 1961, Ranald MacDougall),* Les Films du coeur*, 5 December 1963, p. 27.*

publishing the complete story. It takes only a fraction of a second to turn the page, whereas the temporal gap between question and answer is key to any good cliffhanger. Besides, the reader's knowledge of the story's ending jeopardizes the narrative usefulness of the cliffhanger. One has, therefore, to look for other solutions, as cleverly demonstrated in the film-photonovel version of the Hitchcock movie *Rear Window*.

"La Finestra sul cortile" is in the fifth issue of the *Star Cineromanzo Gigante* series, which ran from 15 March 1955 until June 1956. It was a typical Franco Bozzesi publication, appreciated for the readable inclusion of captions and dialogues in the upper part of the images. The Hitchcock adaptation runs to fifty-eight pages, and the other six pages of the magazine contain a short story, an installment of a serialized novel, film news on all kind of stars, some publicity for other Bozzesi productions, and, on the inside back cover, an astonishing—but, for readers at the time, not unusual—extremely short film-novel adaptation of William Keighley's 1951 *Close to My Heart* in six captioned images. It is significant to note the absence of any reference to Alfred Hitchcock, whose auteur status was still in the future, in these sections. In 1955, the master of suspense was just a Hollywood employee like many others. When "La Finestra sul cortile" was published in French translation a few years later, the relatively low status of the director was highlighted by the fact that the adaptation did not appear in the flagship *Star Ciné Roman* but rather in the smaller (and cheaper) *Les Films pour vous*. The quality of the magazine is rather poor, as is that of the images, clearly copied from the celluloid roll at the end of its first run.

In other film photonovels, it is not difficult to identify the parts and layers of the story that were deleted or added. Such an analysis zooms in on the radically impoverished form and content of the film-photonovel version, which is deprived of any form of irony in order to insist on old-fashioned visions of love and marriage. Almost nothing remains of the subtle wit of most of the dialogue; instead, the omnipresent narrative voice preaches a defense of marital love. At the same time, it is evident that the transmedial adaptation, in spite of the brutal reduction of the film to the basics, manages to create a clear plot. Plot structure is maintained, as is its rhythm: no crucial information is overlooked, and there is a rough match between the number of images and the length of the episodes in the movie. The film photonovel offers a self-enclosed story in which nothing essential to the plot is missing, and it functions as a real double of the film in this regard. It uses key characteristics of the photonovel language and the magazine format in a satisfying way: if the story is told by the (invented) voice-over and the (freely rewritten) dialogue, the images perfectly exploit the aesthetics of the portrait, medium shots, and close-ups. In addition, most panels manage to give a strong sense of the erotic aura of the two stars (Jimmy Stewart and Grace Kelly). The pictures are freed from the logic of mere sequentiality so that they can be reshaped as independent objects with the capacity to represent the whole movie. This narrative paradox, as discussed earlier in this chapter, was disclosed by Victor Burgin in his study on the "remembered film," which is based not on the recalling of actual scenes but on the personal re-creation of stories generated by powerful fixed images (Burgin 2004).

This Bozzesi film photonovel shows how to achieve an expressive transmedial adaptation, both visually and narratively (assuming it is possible to radically separate these two layers). Let us start with the purely visual aspect of the transposition. Although not shot in the subjective point-of-view mode throughout, *Rear Window* rigorously sticks to a single observation point: the apartment of an adventurous photographer, Jeff, confined to a wheelchair after a racetrack accident. The film shows only this apartment, the courtyard, and other apartments visible from Jeff's rear window. When Jeff and his visitors observe the neighborhood, what appears on screen is a multiply fragmented space: the courtyard wall is a surface that is divided into uniform floors, windows, bricks—in short, a space strictly divided along vertical and horizontal lines that transform it into a checkerboard of unequal squares that alternate light and dark colors. The film-photonovel version not only transposes that idea but also reinforces it by intertwining two medium-specific elements. First, "La Finestra sul cortile" creates a direct correspondence among features of the fictional setting, which is horizontally divided into identical floors and vertically segmented by similar windows divided into panes that are further divided by sliding jalousies, turning each window into a miniature version of this global structure. The structure of the page layout demonstrates a rigid composition of identical tiers segmented into similarly sized panels, giving us a family resemblance between the film photonovel and the checkerboard-like film setting. In the movie, the small differences of the apartment and the wall seen through the rear window, repeated over and over again, match the panel division of the page.

The layout in figure 5.6, apparently uneventful, shows examples of such matches: the steps of the staircase (panel 2); the paved tiles in the garden and the vertical bars of the fence (panel 3); the shelves to the right of Jeff's desk (panels 1 and 4); and the juxtaposition of pictures on the wall (panels 5 and 6). All these elements shape a permanently moving fictional double of the underlying grid. Moreover, this basic grid, common to the fictional world of the apartment's wall and the material world of the magazine

FIGURE 5.6. *"La Finestra sul cortile" (*Rear Window, *1954, Alfred Hitchcock),* Star Cineromanzo Gigante, *30 June 1955, p. 3.*

page, is highlighted by the introduction of a second grid structure, that of the captions and dialogues. In "Finestra sul cortile," the words appear in similar places in each panel, and chromatically, they are strongly contrasted—they appear as either white on dark surfaces or black on light surfaces—and this disparity helps produce the visual perception of a second lattice spread over the grid structure of the page and the fictional grid-like motifs.

This composition is powerful because it translates the fictional setting of *Rear Window* into a set of fundamental page layout principles in addition to capturing the intrinsic dynamism of the filmic image. Indeed, Jeff's observations are not static: his gaze is permanently panning and tilting—a gesture to its cinematographic origin—and it is enhanced by visual devices, such as binoculars and a camera with a telephoto lens. True, the static nature of the fixed images and the rigid page layout of the film photonovel cannot compete with Hitchcock's dynamic filmmaking. But, the maker of "La Finestra sul cortile" nevertheless manages to produce similar effects of mobility and dynamism. Several techniques are used to create this impression of motion and agility. First, there is a systematic use of changes in panel size: in principle, each double spread contains one "divergent" panel, either a panoramic image that fills a complete tier, or a small vertical image that constitutes a kind of column on the left or right of the double spread. Second, there is the frequent disruption of elementary eye-match rules, the gaze of the characters not being directed toward the object they are looking at. Third, there is the tension between the linear structure of the panel composition (in principle it is always possible to read from left to right, tier after tier) and the tabular, that is tableau-like, structure of each panel taken as a single composition (each page is clearly meant to make visible a certain number of matches and differences between visual parameters, which are structured at page level, not at image level). These techniques and others produce a creative tension between the utter rigidity of the basic grid structures and the subtle mobility encouraged by the concrete implementation of these rules in images and page layouts that force the reader's gaze to browse the page in all directions. The reader, beyond having an interest in the plot, is able to embrace Jeff's way of looking, which is both focused and multidirectional.

The migration from film to film photonovel not only produces challenging effects at a visual level but also with regard to medium-specific narrative values. A good example here is the page that summarizes the final struggle of Jeff and Thorwald (fig. 5.7), the murderer who Jeff first observed and then unmasked and who enters Jeff's unlocked apartment to kill him. In comparison with the cinematographic version of this scene,

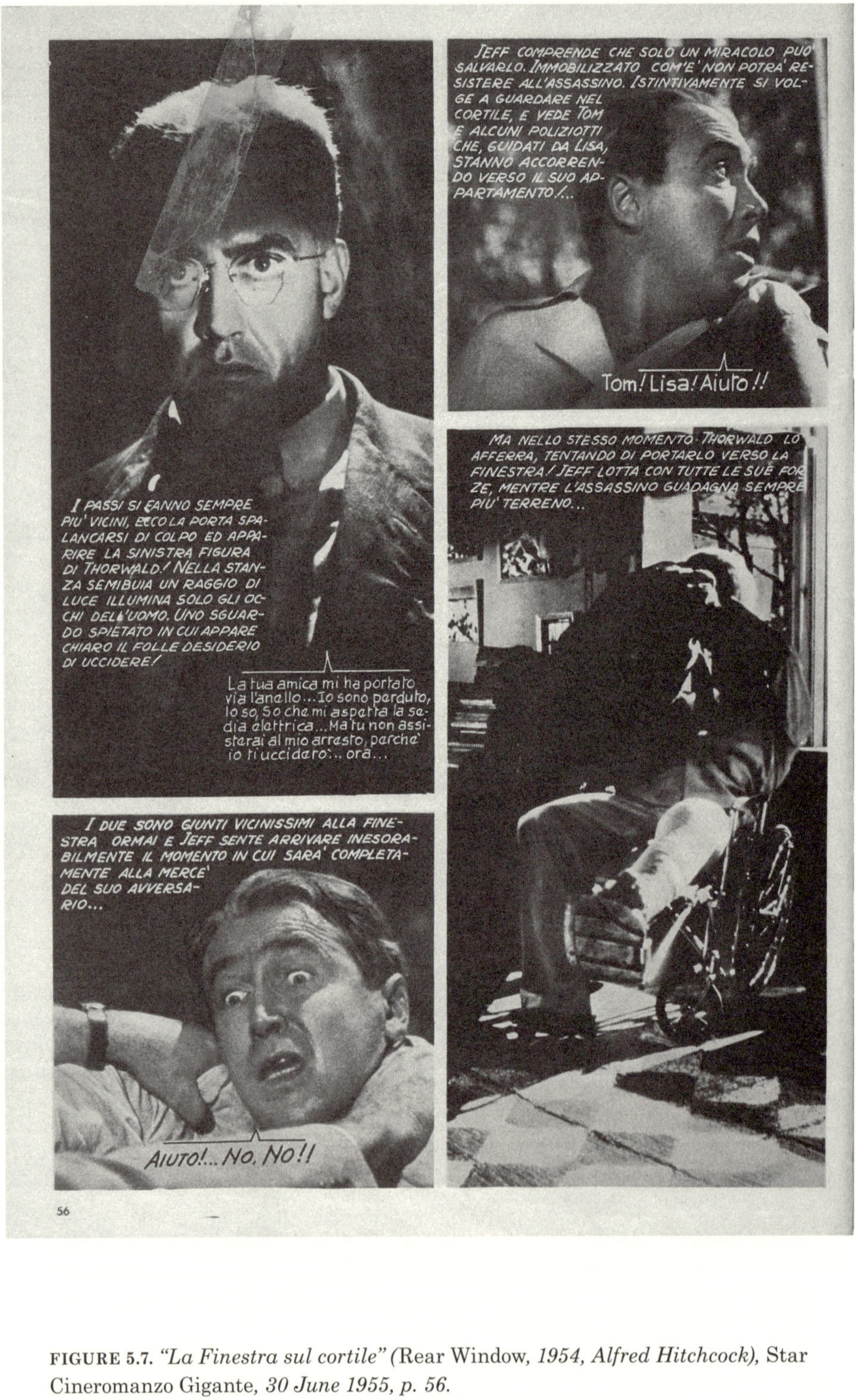

FIGURE 5.7. *"La Finestra sul cortile" (*Rear Window, *1954, Alfred Hitchcock),* Star Cineromanzo Gigante, *30 June 1955, p. 56.*

a masterpiece of suspense and filmic intelligence, the treatment in "La Finestra sul cortile" seems ridiculously shallow and disappointing. But the comparison misses a crucial point, namely, the film photonovel's attempt to create an equally clever and well-made composition that achieves the idea of the struggle between life and death via the means of production that the film photonovel offers.

More specifically, the narrative effect here is not the result of a cliff-hanger (since everybody knows how the story ends) but of other elements. The unusual layout, with only four panels (the only instance of this in the whole story), reshapes the temporal succession of this plot moment into a single spatial composition. Any form of linear reading is disrupted, paradoxically, by a sequence implementing a mechanism of suspense: the images on this page are meant to be read not one after another but rather next to one another; it is physically impossible not to see the last image when discovering the first one. Tension at the content level is replaced by visual contrasts: clashes between small and large panels, between dark and light parts of text and image, between shot and reverse shot, between close-up and medium shot, between the orientation of the gaze to left and right, and so on.

None of these elements copy what happens in Hitchcock's movie, but the way in which "La Finestra sul cortile" implements them in a different medium demonstrates what film photonovels can do. Once again, it is crucial to underline that the success of the adaptation also depends on its refusal to directly compete with Hitchcock's original. Readers who knew *Rear Window* would realize that the film photonovel version, which was evidently meant to serve as a substitute for the no-longer-available movie, nonetheless had to be read as an autonomous work. The stakes of such a perspectival shift are high, but so are its rewards.

Is There a Fourth Wall in the Room?

In the film photonovel, everything is a double from the start. The story is an adaptation of an existing one. The images are film stills or set pictures (the latter often already known from other publication venues): pinup photography, publicity images, and press illustrations. At the same time, no film photonovel is ever a true reproduction (if such a thing is even possible). The storytelling techniques unite word and image in new ways—a voice-over with a focus on simultaneous narration provides a different take on time. And the images in the magazines have been selected, recropped, and edited according the rules of the film-photonovel magazine, which requires a radical reframing to highlight melodrama and celebrity culture.

The specific features of the film photonovel as a narrative genre have a large impact on the types of images that are chosen and how they are used. Film-photonovel images are different from similar images in the original movie, even if they pretend to be faithful copies, and they are edited differently from those used in photonovels and film novels. In the rest of this chapter, I illustrate this difference in two ways: first, by analyzing a general visual stereotype, the "direct address" shot; and second, by a close reading of an intriguing case of internal repetition, evinced by the multiple reuse of similar photographs within the same film photonovel.

Relying on the protocols found in continuity editing, which tends to make the presence of the camera as unobtrusive as possible, classic narrative cinema generally avoids shots in which the fictional characters directly look into the camera. This direct-address technique, which works to break the illusionistic fourth wall, is shunned or, more precisely, restricted to specific situations that tend to neutralize and psychologically motivate the rupture of the referential illusion. (An exception: shots in which actors look into the camera by accident and the scene could not be deleted or reshot.) There are three major uses of the direct-address technique. First, it engenders complicity with the spectator, as in many Laurel and Hardy sketches or certain Woody Allen movies, increasing the intended effect of the comedy, a genre with a relaxed and liberal attitude toward realism. Second, it corresponds to and returns the subjective point-of-view shot in which the filmed image is presented as the subjective view of a character—the character looking at the camera is then supposed to look at the character whose gaze directs the viewer to the point-of-view shot—an instance in which the direct-address technique is realistically motivated.

Finally, direct address provokes a demand for empathy, as in the famous final sequence of Truffaut's *The 400 Blows* (1959), in which the protagonist, Antoine Doinel, stares intensely into the camera. This freeze-frame constitutes the final shot of the work: when Antoine stops running and turns his gaze to the camera, the image suddenly freezes, the camera rapidly zooms in on Antoine's face, and the word "fin" ("The End") appears in large white capital letters over the whole width of the screen. This particular treatment of the direct address as a special transition between the fictional status of the movie and the nonfictional status of the final credits likewise makes the direct-address technique plausible. The audience is not simply asked to identify with the adolescent—after all, the whole movie is constructed to make this call for identification almost self-evident—but also to transfer its (brief?) sympathy for Antoine to a sustainable sympathy in real life. Truffaut's film forces us to become aware of our responsibility for "lost youths" such as Antoine Doinel, both during the projection of the film and after leaving the theater. More generally, the director invites us to change our attitude toward movies, which, for him and his fellow New Wave practitioners, are more than just entertainment.

The direct-address technique of *The 400 Blows* not only bridges the gap between art and life but also highlights the difference between theater and film, a medium intended to supersede the intrinsic limitations of the spectacle culture denounced by Jean-Jacques Rousseau in his famous *Letter to M. d'Alembert on the Theater* (1758):

> If [. . .] the heart is more touched by feigned ills than by real ones, if theatrical imitations draw forth more tears than would the presence of the objects imitated, it is less because the emotions are feebler and do not reach the level of pain [. . .], than because they are pure and without mixture of anxiety for ourselves. In giving our tears to these fictions, we have satisfied all the rights of humanity without having to give anything more of ourselves; whereas unfortunate people in person would require attention from us, relief, consolation, and work, which would involve us in their pains and would require at least the sacrifice of our indolence, from all of which we are content to be exempt. It could be said that our heart closes itself for fear of being touched at our expense. (Rousseau [1758] 1968, 25; ellipsis added)

Identification, empathy, and solidarity: these words do not sound hollow in the melodramatic context of the film photonovel. And it is certainly true that direct-address shots abound in the genre. Their meaning, however, is far from being comparable to that of the corresponding movie images. This kind of panel does not have the same disruptive impact as similar film images. In the film photonovel, the reader does not have the impression that looking directly at the camera breaks any rule, certainly not the rule of the fourth wall.

Film photonovels are made of printed photographs, a clear link with portrait photography. Portrait photography, which is typically a nonfiction genre, lacks a prohibition on direct-address shots. In the context of the magazines, portraits are inevitably found in celebrity and pinup photography, two genres in which looking at the camera is anything but exceptional. The relative banality of this kind of shot thus implies that film photonovels will naturally exploit the special status of these shots. But the direct-address technique will never have the same result in the film photonovel as in its filmic counterpart.

A good example of these limits can be found in *Rear Window*. In the movie, the self-representative aesthetics have been studied in great detail, and Hitchcock cleverly teases the audience with the first screen appearance of Grace Kelly as Lisa Fremont. When she surprises the slumbering James Stewart (Jeff), the words she whispers are the first shot in direct-address mode in the movie, and this shot breaks the rules in more than one way. Jeff is asleep—unless the shot suggests that he is only faking—but since the whole film elaborates on the metaphorical relationship between character, director, and spectator, as well as on the many uses of the point-of-view shot, we suspect that Kelly is really returning Stewart's subjective shot and that she is really looking at him, that is, at us spectators and not at the camera, which is supposed to remain invisible. Obviously, the lack of verisimilitude of the filmic montage puts forward the idea that what Grace Kelly is looking at is also the camera and thus the director, and not just Stewart or the spectators in the theater. Kelly's first direct-address appearance can thus be understood as an ironic, possibly even sadistic hint from the director to the spectator, as if the former was murmuring to the latter: dear spectator, don't believe that you "are" the Jimmy Stewart character, for he will get the girl and you will get nothing.

Given the difference in the status and function of the direct address in the two media, the film-photonovel version of this scene cannot engage the spectator as suggestively as the movie images. But its page layout definitely succeeds in displaying a subtle shock effect as similar as it is dissimilar to what happens on screen (see fig. 5.8). After eight pages in which the characters hide their gazes and shy away from any direct eye contact with the reader—and as already mentioned, the frequent shifts in distance and direction as well as the play with mismatched eyelines draw attention to the motif and structure of the gaze—a direct address suddenly appears that disrupts the continuity of the editing principles in a twofold way. First, the Grace Kelly picture (panel 3) transgresses the prohibition on looking at the camera (a tiny transgression in the film-photonovel universe). Second, the following image, in which the look of James Stewart shifts from a traditional representation (panel 2) to a nearly direct-address representation (panel 4), can be interpreted by the reader as an image that simultaneously follows and precedes panel 3. It follows it, since Grace Kelly's whispering voice wakes up the sleeping Stewart. But it paradoxically precedes it, for this is the only way to realistically explain the direct address in panel 3 as an answer to an implicit subjective shot. The film-photonovel montage is simple but smart, and it facilitates the creative possibilities of spatial arrangements and the ways those arrangements make the classic rules of temporal montage less dominant and less linear.

FIGURE 5.8. *"La Finestra sul cortile"* (Rear Window, *1954, Alfred Hitchcock),* Star Cineromanzo Gigante, *30 June 1955, p. 9.*

Twice-Told Tales

Distinguishing between film-still pictures and set pictures is both easy and demanding. In general, set pictures as they appear in the magazine are of higher quality. Their resolution is higher, and they resemble posed photographs more than excerpts from film reels. In principle, it is possible to compare the images in a film photonovel with those of the movie: set pictures are never exactly the same as those shot for the movie. Finally, set pictures are often intrinsically different: they are celebrity pictures, with the stars posing between takes, or *tableau vivant*–like compositions with the actors reenacting, for a staged photograph, the take just recorded. But set pictures are sometimes badly printed, and at times the original shot or movie might not be available for comparison. Some films disappear, one of the reasons why the public was keen on buying film photonovels. Certain shots or sequences may have been dropped during editing but are eventually recuperated in the film-photonovel version. Moreover, it is not difficult to imagine or remember scenes or movies whose aesthetic programs were close to that of posing. But even then, other aspects can be taken into account to help interpret the specific nature of the images used in the film photonovel. It can be enough to know the specific policy of a magazine regarding the question of film stills versus set pictures.

The real question is not related to the material distinction between film stills and set pictures but rather to the challenges and opportunities raised by the preference for set pictures. Although this model, at first sight, seems to involve the stiffest constraints, the aesthetic superiority of set pictures seems overruled by an almost insurmountable handicap: the limited number and availability of these kinds of pictures, which were used to illustrate film novels, too. In most cases, film novels required only a small number of illustrations, which may not have been enough to tell the story well. The film photonovel, by contrast, contained an average of 300 pictures, which allowed for the story to develop smoothly.

The hostile reactions to a magazine such as *Amor Film* can partly be explained by the use of too few images, but the most obvious counterexample is *Elevator to the Gallows* (*Ascenseur pour l'échafaud*), a 1958 thriller by Louis Malle inspired by a 1956 novel of the same name by the French noir author Noël Calef. In this story, two lovers decide to kill the woman's husband, but their story does not end well. After the "perfect" murder, the hero (or antihero) is trapped in an elevator and cannot produce a plausible alibi for a second murder, of which he is wrongly accused. Most people today remember the movie for the haunting score composed and executed by Miles Davis. But it is unfair to isolate the soundtrack from the rest of the work, a key movie in the emergence of New Wave cinema.

The movie powerfully reduced the adapted novel to its essence, and the movie was then remade even more concisely as a film photonovel, which benefited from the medium's minimalism. The film photonovel exists in two versions, one published almost immediately after the release of the film, another published two years later (the publication of the same work in different magazines was not exceptional in the film-photonovel genre). The former is an eight-page short-story version strongly influenced by the short film novelizations and the photonovels published in the same magazine: *Ciné-Révélation*. The later adaptation is a complete-story version published in *Mon Film*, the magazine that most consistently combined the key rules of the genre (a three-by-two grid, approximately fifty pages and three hundred images, a voice-over, a focus on image panels, few all-text panels) and a house style based on the exclusive use of set pictures. The magazine also featured a somewhat crude but efficient and recognizable treatment of captions and dialogue, always printed on the images themselves and always framed in text balloons with black letters on white surfaces.

The *Mon Film* version uses the same pictures as the *Ciné-Révélation* short story. Of the 96 images in the earlier version (which includes 11 text panels), only 19 (20 percent of the total) were not recuperated in the later version. This extreme degree of reuse can only hint at the quantitative limitations of the material available: if there had been more set pictures, the later version would probably not have been obliged to reuse approximately 80 percent of the first picture set. The fact that only 19 pictures of the original version were not recycled makes another aspect of the second version even more remarkable. In *Mon Film*, many images are not shown once, but twice, thrice, and even four times. This internal reduplication is the direct and inexorable consequence of the lack of sufficient visual resources and the necessity of following a particular publication format. *Mon Film* film photonovels contain approximately 50 pages, each page composed of 6 pictures similarly sized; moreover, the magazine does not include full-page images and uses relatively few text panels. "Elevator to the Gallows" is a 50-page work with 286 image panels, 87 of which are duplicated images.

The ways in which many images are recycled via adaptation represents a potential constraint within the genre. This constraint can work in two ways: as something that cripples the elaboration of the work or as the mother of new and interesting inventions. In the *Mon Film* version, invention clearly has the upper hand. The film photonovel succeeds in establishing techniques and patterns of repetition that make the recycling almost invisible to the average reader, who is mostly interested in the major plot points. Even if these recycled images are detected, the recycling techniques do not necessarily hinder the reader's pleasure, for they are not experienced as a flaw but as an invitation to enjoy the resourcefulness that they represent.

In practice, at least five techniques are deployed in the metamorphosis of the perception of the recycled images, making them appear to be "new" images in each instance. The first technique is the simultaneous use of nearly similar images in certain sequences—the small differences between these pictures ensure that the reader does not immediately notice the absence of differences between images in other sequences, which are deciphered as being comparable to other similar images. A second aspect is the extreme narrative tension created almost from the very first panel—the pace of storytelling is breathtaking, and the more the reader is captured by the plot, the easier it is for him or her to overlook certain material elements of the work, such as the recycling of images. Much attention is given to the dialogue, which tends to diminish the relative importance of the accompanying images—since the short, sharp dialogue drives the story with extreme speed, the reader is not tempted to look carefully at the details of the talking heads that compose most of the work. The small number of pictures per page and the crispness of the text snippets strongly participate in the creation of a reading protocol based on suspense and the desire to know how it all will end. The position of captions and speech balloons may change, and this alteration generally suffices to transform images repeated in two panels: the visually different relationships between word and image induce a reading mode that deciphers two panels with changing word-and-image combinations as two dissimilar panels, even when the images do not change. Finally, and this technique is perhaps the most far-reaching one, *Mon Film* takes great care to introduce small variations within the recycled images: repeated images do not reappear in the same row or column, or on the same page, and repeated images are recropped, either to highlight a detail or to contextualize a particular aspect of the narrative. And all these mechanisms are mixed and remixed so that the recycling of images is, at a glance, imperceptible to the reader.

We can turn to pages 38 and 39, for example (the pagination starts on page 3), where we find an image repeated four times (panels 2, 3, 4, and 5, page 38; see fig. 5.9), immediately followed by the repetition of an image that looks nearly identical (panels 2 and 3 of the following page). The pervasive presence of this picture is toned down by the convergent impacts of all the techniques mentioned above: the near repetition in panels 1 and 2, which contain only small differences (the almost perfect repetition of the same image four times, for example); the use of a climactic scene (it is

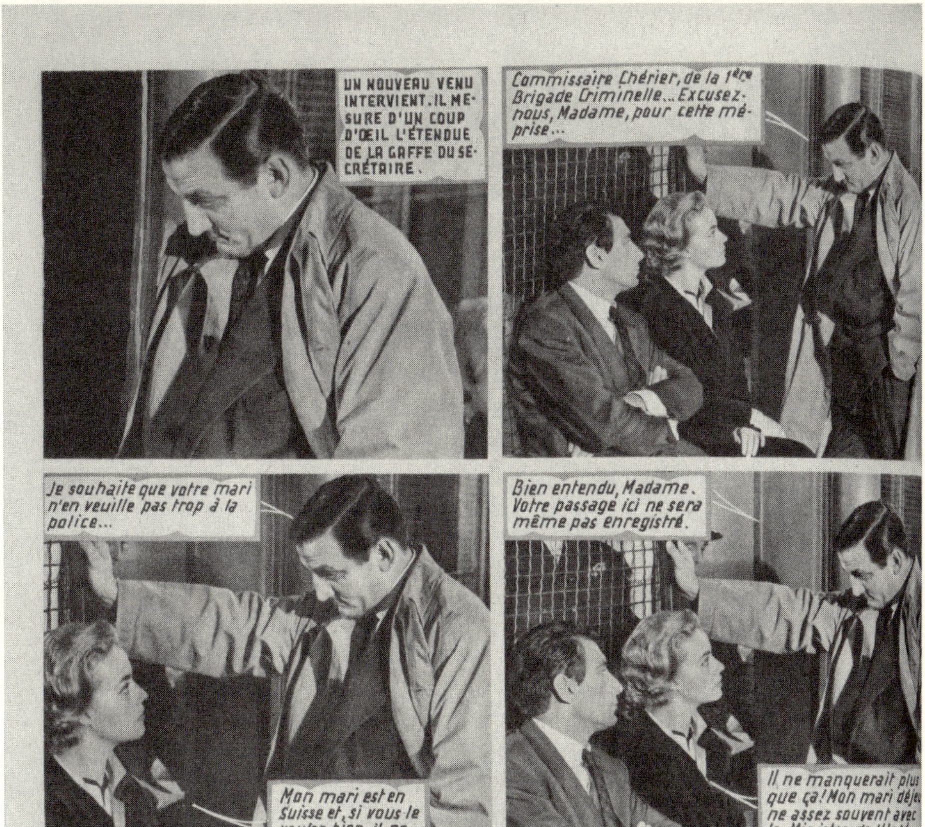

FIGURE 5.9. *"Ascenseur pour l'échafaud" (*Ascenseur pour l'échafaud*, 1958, Louis Malle),* Mon Film*, October 1960, p. 38.*

the first appearance of the police detective, so readers realize that things are getting serious) and a plot twist that pushes reader to continue reading; the inclusion of voluminous dialogue, which diverts attention from the image (moreover, it is not implausible to think that the characters barely move while talking); the ever-shifting layout of the captions, speech balloons, and text panels, which mitigate the static aspect of the pictures; and most importantly, the transition from one repeated image to another (though the repetition is never completely literal: images change places in the rows and columns, they are recropped to suggest a zooming in or a zooming out, and so on). Less is undoubtedly more, and the narrative efficiency of the *Mon Film* version is evident.

6 / Globalizing the Film Photonovel?

The film photonovel was big in Italy for some years and for a slightly longer time in France. There were some examples in Spain and the United Kingdom, all of them short-lived and not nearly as commercially successful as their Franco-Italian peers. What about the rest of the world, particularly the Americas?[1] *Fotonovelas* are tremendously successful not only in Mexico, where their history and social impact have been well documented (Herner 1979; Curiel 1990), but also in countries such as Argentina and Chile.[2] Moreover, the pervasive presence of Hollywood in postwar Latin America is evident in the work of novelists such as Manuel Puig, the Argentinean author of *Betrayed by Rita Hayworth* (1968) and *Kiss of the Spider Woman* (1976). South America thus seems like it should have been a hotbed for a blossoming local film-photonovel industry in conjunction with imported European works. Such an arrangement could have been facilitated by the binational structure of many publishing companies, such as Editorial Molino (Barcelona and Buenos Aires), whose book series *Biblioteca de Oro* was a key publisher in the field of popular fiction.

Despite this theoretically favorable context for the emergence of global forms of the film photonovel in Latin America, actual production remained limited. Herner (1979, 25) mentions two early examples published in the Mexican magazine *Pinocho*: "Lágrimas de antaño" (1943; based on *Now, Voyager*, Irving Rapper, 1942) and "Doña Bárbara" (1944; based on the Mexican film of the same name, directed by Fernando de Fuentes and Miguel M. Delgado, 1943). These can be considered Mexican forerunners of the film photonovel, but Herner does not provide any details or illustrations. It is therefore difficult to say whether these two publications were real film photonovels or rather variations on the illustrated novelization, a confusion of genre that is widespread in scholarship in this field. Whatever these two publications may have been, they were clearly one-shots, not the result of an editorial policy to open a new niche.

When film photonovels emerged in magazines in Latin America many years later, the influence of Italian or French models was obvious. But in all cases, the number of magazines and issues seems to have been rather small, and the same can be said of the lifespans of these magazines: sticking closely to the European model but focusing on US and Mexican movies, *SuperAventuras* was active in the early 1960s; *Cine Aventuras* had a much longer career, but the adaptations it contained followed the prototype of the captioned film novel, a film retold in film stills with captions instead of balloons, arranged in a purely mechanical page layout. In their study of the South American photonovel, Carrillo and Lyson (1983) mention some "real" film photonovels based on the hybridization of comics and photonovels, but the authors give no further details. Finally, there were some film photonovels, probably translated from Italian, in Argentinean photonovel magazines such as *Secretos: Amiga y confidente de la mujer*, which ran this kind of material in the late 1950s.[3] But all in all, the production levels were not comparable to what was happening in Europe in the same period, though the rediscovery of a hidden continent is never to be dismissed.

The situation in the United States was both similar and different. The country has never produced a real equivalent of the European or Latin American film photonovel. The reasons for this absence are twofold. First, American adoption of television was widespread by the time film photonovels came into vogue in Europe, where the success of the film photonovel was largely a pretelevision phenomenon. Once television sets penetrated private homes in Europe, the film photonovel suddenly disappeared—a phenomenon sharply observed by authors such as Italo Calvino (quoted in Morreale 2011, 279), in terms that reveal nostalgia for the fading of a popular culture predating the rise of mass-media culture in general. Second, US culture is always open to the input of non-US creators, but was rather reluctant, to put it mildly, to adopt non-US cultural products and industries in the period under scrutiny. Instead of importing a work, a format, or a medium, American cultural industries prefer local remakes. This structural threshold to the translation of European models undoubtedly hindered the export of the Franco-Italian film-photonovel format to the United States. This lack of export success was not due to any insurmountable exoticism of the product. American publications retold films with the help of publicity shots or film stills in formats such as the illustrated summaries and short novelizations found in specialized film fan magazines as well as in general-interest magazines such as *Life*, already active in this field in the 1940s.

At the same time, the United States played a crucial role in the invention of three subgenres (or derived forms) that extended the scope of the film photonovel. Despite the relatively marginal position of each of these forms, which roughly correspond to the classic distinction between lowbrow, middlebrow, and highbrow, the influence of the US examples and experiments was key to the development of the genre.

The first specifically US contribution to the field is *Famous Films*, a magazine created by James Warren in 1964. Inspired by EC's horror comics (and after unsuccessfully attempting to imitate *Playboy*), Warren launched the first of a wide range of horror magazines in 1958, a publication format that escaped Comics Code regulations by virtue of its size; the code applied only to the small-format comic books. Warren's publications included *Famous Monsters of Filmland*, *Creepy*, *Eerie*, *Vampirella*, and the like. Warren Publications went bankrupt in the early 1980s. Most of its magazines had a strong relationship with the fan culture around horror movies. *Famous Films* represents the film-photonovel turn in the publisher's catalogue. The back cover of the magazine announced, "2 all new film stories—told in 500 photos—in one magazine—an entirely NEW adventure in monstrous, exciting reading!" *Famous Films* abandoned the tradition of the illustrated novelization, adopting the typical page layout and narrative techniques of photonovels and comics (see fig. 6.1), although in a short-story format (the "500 photos" announced in the blurb is a gross exaggeration: "Curse of Frankenstein," for instance, published in issue 2, has only 74 pictures, and "Horror of Dracula," published in the same issue, has 80 pictures).

It is not a stretch to claim that *Famous Films* is a US remake based on the European format. The hypothesis makes sense, but does not do justice to the undeniable originality of the Warren magazine. It is worthwhile to advance a more complex genealogy. Warren Publications also issued *HELP!* (1960–1965), a satirical magazine created by Harvey Kurtzman after he left *MAD* and EC and whose major innovation was the parody of other magazines, films, and television shows, often using a *fumetti* or photonovel format (a tradition that was continued in the single-page "funny stories" of

FIGURE 6.1. *"The Curse of Frankenstein" (*The Curse of Frankenstein*, 1957, Terence Fisher),* Famous Films #2 *(actually #3), 1965, p. 32.*

National Lampoon, a humor magazine (1970–1978) created after *HELP!*). *HELP!*, whose editorial history has some connections with Europe (Labarre 2017), introduced the photonovel genre in the US magazine market, but radically changed its form and content. While the European photonovel was, at least in these years, still profoundly integrated with the romance publishing business, the *HELP! fumetti* were exclusively satirical and self-reflexive (it was a medium taking other media as both its subject and its target). Moreover, *HELP!*'s visual and narrative strategies were not those of serialized storytelling but of the illustrated short story or sketch, with frequent borrowings from typical comics conventions, such as large handwritten onomatopoetic words, all of which can be directly traced back to *Famous Films*. Finally, the page layout of Warren's film-photonovel magazine was more diverse and expressive than those of the European works. In *Famous Films*, no underlying three-by-two grid serves as an implicit model; each page has a different layout, and the shock effect of the individual photos is strongly underlined (this shock effect is, of course, not to be taken at face value, since horror fans are perfectly aware of the genre codes).

Famous Films is an original contribution to the poetics of the film photonovel. It explores aspects and tendencies that came to the fore only in later transformations. It appeared at the moment of the shift from general publications (in magazines addressing a large audience and retelling any kind of movie) to lowbrow niche productions, characterized by a more eccentric and caricatured style. This exaggerated style was, for instance, how spaghetti westerns were often treated between 1965 and 1975, after the collapse of the classic film-photonovel magazines. *Famous Films* was short-lived, and information on the series is scarce: the "about" page for the Warren Publishing Archive (2011) in the Internet Archive does not mention it specifically, labeling the second issue of the series, "The Mole People," as "miscellaneous." The *Warren Companion* is more precise: "The title used the Italian fumetti approach to comics, i.e., utilizing film stills instead of line drawn artwork to tell the story. As its title suggests, *Famous Films* adapted one or two movies in each issue. None of the issues were dated except for a copyright notice of 1964, but from advertisements in other Warren titles an approximate chronology has been established (bearing in mind that the cover date is always several months ahead of its actual newsstand appearance)" (Cooke and Roach 2001, 219). The *Companion* lists three issues: "The Horror of Party Beach" (issue 1, November 1964), "The Mole People" (issue 2, January 1965), and "Curse of Frankenstein / Horror of Dracula" (despite being numbered issue 2, the *Companion* identifies it as issue 3, March 1965). The short-lived nature and limited circulation (mainly in horror fan communities) of *Famous Films* seem to exclude the idea that the magazine exerted some direct influence on later changes to the film photonovel in Europe, but it cannot be denied that the magazine played a pioneering role in the broadening of the genre.

Almost as forgotten as the *Famous Films* experiment is an innovation concerning a special type of film and television adaptation during the second half of the 1970s. Several series of American pocketbooks were marketed as "photonovels" or "photostories"—a somewhat deceptive label for what were actually film photonovels in book format. This new type of film photonovel, the first to leave the world of magazine publishing, appeared in the slipstream of the period's science fiction boom, but it quickly disappeared after the introduction of affordable VCR technology and home video in the early 1980s. It can be defined as a middlebrow version of Warren Publications' stories told with pictures. Many of the films and TV serials that were adapted did not belong to the niche of monster and horror movies but cashed in on the immensely popular genre of science fiction (*Star Wars* was released in 1977). In practice, the publication policy of these series was rather eclectic: next to *Close Encounters of the Third Kind* (1977), *Invasion of the Body Snatchers* (1978), *Alien* (1979—a large-format book), and many other sci-fi works (*Star Trek* was, of course, on top, represented by two films and twelve television episodes), there were also adaptations of *Nashville* (1975), *Grease* (1978), *Hair* (1979), and *Rocky* (1979). The middlebrow dimension of this new publishing phenomenon was due not only to the shift from magazine to (pocket) book but also to a closer link with the official novelization and tie-in industry, which developed strongly in this period. The link with juvenile fan culture remained strong, however, as shown by several fan sites that look back nostalgically on these books. Here is John Kenneth Muir (2005):

> Before TiVo, before DVD box sets, before VCRs even, the intrepid genre fan really had to do some deep searching to find good ways (other than catching the right rerun . . .) to relive his favorite episodes of *Star Trek*, or a favorite genre movie like *Alien*. There were comic book adaptations, of course, and lavishly illustrated storybooks (the subject of a future flashback here!) and even novelizations. However, once upon a time, there was also another great avenue in which to relive your favorite production, the strange and unusual collectible known as . . . a *photonovel*.
>
> Now, I have to say, I grew up with photonovels, and I love them with a passion. I'm sure there are elitists out there who say that photonovels are basically nothing but elaborate picture books, but I would counter that they are much more than that. I have always believed that film and TV are first and foremost visual art forms. That the images we

> see, and *how we see them*, tell us as much about a story (if not more . . .) than dialogue does. After all, without visuals, film and TV are simply . . . radio (which is way cool too; but a totally different medium). The great thing about photonovels is that they re-capture the images of a particular film or TV episode and re-tell the story in a kindred fashion, in *images* (with cartoon balloons in some cases, like comic-books, providing the pertinent dialogue).

Despite this tight connection with the world of adolescent subculture, the cultural upgrade of the film photonovel to the book medium is highly relevant. Moreover, most of these publications were in full color, with a layout that was less influenced by models borrowed from comics and *fumetti*. Instead, there was an attempt to produce less repetitive combinations of words and images, as well as to produce—and no longer simply reproduce—a medium-specific experience of the original movie.

Perhaps the most astonishing work of this period is the six-page wordless film-photonovel adaptation that was part of the printed but never distributed book *The Bonnie and Clyde Scrapbook*.[4] Here are some excerpts from the story of this exceptional film-photo short story, as told by its noncredited author, Bhob Stewart (1937–2014, a writer and active fan, probably best known as a film columnist for *Heavy Metal*):

> I designed the Krigstein-influenced pages above as a section in *The Bonnie and Clyde Scrapbook*, published by Personality Posters in 1968. The story behind the creation of this book might be just as interesting as the book itself. [. . .]
>
> Arthur Penn's *Bonnie and Clyde* was released in August 1967. I must have seen it that fall, and a few months later I read *The True Story of Bonnie and Clyde as Told By Bonnie's Mother and Clyde's Sister* (Signet, 1968), a reprint of Jan Fortune's *Fugitives: The Story of Clyde Barrow and Bonnie Parker* (1934). This book and the movie made me aware that Bonnie Parker had kept a scrapbook of newspaper clippings about the escapes of the Barrow gang from the law. It occurred to me that a facsimile of her scrapbook would make an interesting book, and I decided to present the idea to Woody Gelman, the publisher of Nostalgia Press. [. . .]
>
> Barbara Gelman took that presentation and went out to pitch the book. Despite the success of the movie, no one was interested. As I recall, she was rejected by nine publishers. However, at that time, Personality Posters was hot, and their posters were everywhere. [. . .]
>
> A stack of 1930s news photos was acquired by Barbara from the stock photo service, Black Star. I decided the book needed *Bonnie and Clyde*

> movie stills. I went to the Warner Bros. offices at 666 Fifth Avenue and met with the head publicist who listened with interest as I explained what we were doing. He went away and came back carrying a huge binder with all the photo prints grommeted together. He told me to write down numbers of the stills I wanted, and I gave him a list with 70 numbers. When I went back to Warner Bros., they handed me a manila envelope filled with prints of all the stills I had requested. [. . .]
>
> I began designing the page layouts, working my way through the pile of Black Star pictures. Since numbers on the stills from Warner Bros. were shuffled randomly, there was no way to put them in the proper narrative sequence, and I visualized a filmic fumetti.[5]

As shown by figure 6.2, depicting the final shoot-out, this "Bonnie and Clyde" version offers a complex merger of many models: scrapbooks, comics, jigsaw puzzles, poster images, and, although not mentioned by Bhob Stewart, the more innovative page layouts of the pocketbook photos that accompanied film novelizations in these years, as well as high-art historical models; it is almost unthinkable that this adaptation did not take its inspiration from the famous Surrealist collage *Je ne vois pas la [femme] cachée dans la forêt.*[6] Marginalized in a legal limbo for decades until it was disclosed in a blog post by Bhob Stewart in 2010, this stunning example of the film photonovel proves that the genre had started to penetrate larger cultural circles and practices. Additionally, it was open to ambitious and high-art experimentation. The rapid disappearance of film-photonovel versions in book format may have decelerated or hampered this shift from middlebrow to highbrow culture. But the massive presence of film-photonovel books, and the great variety of styles that they allowed, certainly opened new windows, demonstrating that film photonovelizations were no longer limited to magazine formats following the *fumetti* model.

The third and last step in the history of the genre in the United States is a one-shot, but it has proved to be an immediate and complete game changer in global visual culture: the 1993 bilingual adaptation of Chris Marker's *The Jetty* (*La Jetée*, 1962) by the Canadian typographer and designer Bruce Mau. The artistic achievement of this film photonovel has been a source of inspiration for many creators, though less so in the domain of the film photonovel itself, which no longer existed at the time. Instead, the work has been very influential in the rebirth and expansion of the modern photonovel in art photography.[7]

The Jetty is a cult movie by Chris Marker (pseudonym of Christian Bouche-Villeneuve, 1921–2012).[8] Its most salient characteristic is its almost exclusive use of still images, not as a technical gimmick, but as the

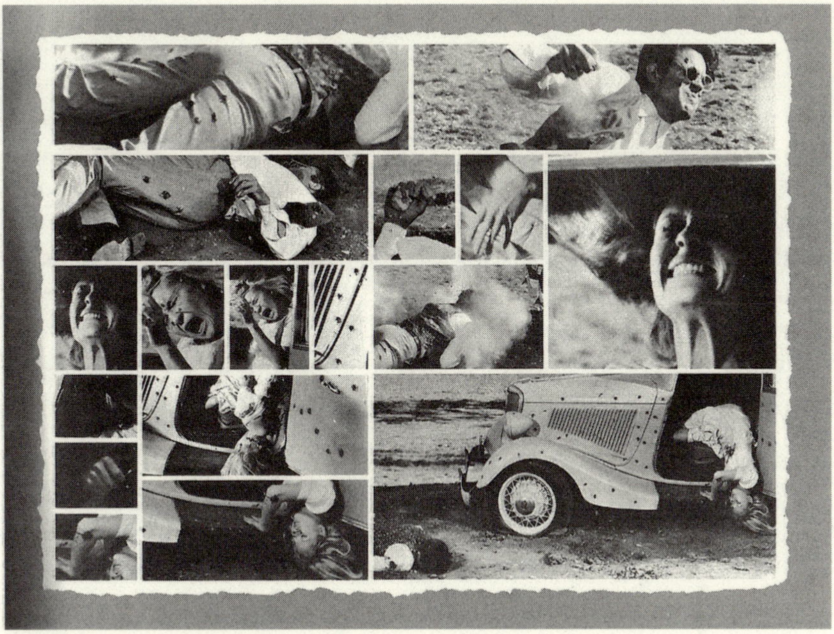

FIGURE 6.2. *Final page of the "Bonnie and Clyde" adaptation by Bhob Stewart, in* The Bonnie and Clyde Scrapbook *(Personality Posters, 1968), n.p.*

filmic counterpart of their aesthetic. The film, a science-fiction-inspired love story, raises philosophical issues related to time and temporality, the nature and power of images, the tension between remembering and invention, and seeing and blindness, among other things. The movie, which is anything but a slide show–*cum*–soundtrack, is labeled a "photonovel" ("*photo-roman*") in the opening credits—a provocative yet understandable decision. By calling his film a photonovel—and we should not forget this genre's execrable reputation in cinephile milieus around 1960—Marker draws attention to the fundamental paradox of cinema, namely, that the art of moving images is based on the rapid projection of fixed images. He also emphasizes the role of montage, which literally takes the place of the moving images in this case. If a viewer of the *The Jetty* is under the impression that he or she is watching a real movie, not a slideshow, it is because of the subtle and intelligent montage techniques of the film.

The film photonovel adaptation of Marker by Mau is as profound and creative as the original movie. At first sight, Mau's intervention seems somewhat minimalist. We see a linear sequence of film stills with the text of the film's voice-over displayed at the bottom of the page. Yet as in the film, this minimalism is a springboard toward a construction of vertiginous complexity. First, Mau reinterprets and redesigns the basic layout and publishing format of the film photonovel in a revolutionary way. Instead of using the traditional vertical format of a magazine or a book, he chose the horizontal (also called "Italian") format, which allows for a better match between filmic and reading experiences, in which the story unfolds image after image. In Mau's version, everything can be read from left to right, all images being displayed one after another, as if it were a movie in print. Moreover, the background color of the gutter and the margins is not white, the default option in almost all film photonovels, but dark blue, almost black: this color, which contrasts with the black-and-white images of the movie, perfectly evokes the theatrical experience of seeing the images on-screen, with dark space surrounding the projected frames.

Once established, this robust but open correspondence between film and book allows Mau to concentrate on a limited set of visual features whose simple, but almost infinite, combinations reshape the montage effects pursued by Marker, in medium-specific ways: the size of the images; the relationship between images and gutter or margins; the presence or absence of captions; and the number of photos per page. The result is simultaneously humble and overwhelming, exactly like the film. A publication of Zone Books, an imprint of MIT Press, *The Jetty* marks a dramatic shift in cultural status (which does not mean that the aspiration to culturally upgrade the initially lowbrow form of the film photonovel is the only meaningful way to address the genre). After the sci-fi pocketbooks of the mid-1970s, this signaled a cultural revolution more or less comparable to what happened to the equally despised photonovel when conceptual and minimalist art photography became interested in staged photography and sequential narrative. Photographers transferred techniques and insights from the lowbrow world of magazine publications and documentary photography to the highbrow and posh world of the art gallery and the museum circuit (the examples of Duane Michals, Sol LeWitt, and James Coleman come here to mind). Yet thanks to the host medium of the book, all these experiments have been able to find their way to a larger audience while leaving many traces in photography and hybridized forms of writing. The film photonovel was not reinvented or rejuvenated by *The Jetty*, which is definitely too sophisticated to convince cultural entrepreneurs to reboot the genre in the age of digital cinema. But the work unquestionably remains a landmark publication in the field, and as shown by the increasing amount of scholarship on Marker, its influence can be seen in many other forms of film novelizations: video art, installations, photo narratives, and novelizations in poetry.

Appendix: Publishers and Magazines

The following list does not claim to be exhaustive. It is limited to a certain type of film photonovel (the typical film photonovel as studied in this book, which differs from illustrated film novels and so-called photonovel versions of film published in pocket-book format), a certain period (the golden age of the traditional film photonovel), a certain geographic and linguistic area (Europe), a publication format (magazines, not one-shot publications), and a certain type of product (roughly speaking, works that were for sale at newsstands; niche categories such as the porn film photonovel, which was sold in sex shops, have not been taken into account). Dates of first and last publication have been checked as closely as possible, but further archival research will undoubtedly help complete and fine-tune this material. The order is alphabetical, not chronological.

France

Main source: personal website of Serge Ghera, http://bmania.pagesperso-orange.fr/index.html.

ARTIMA (AFTER 1962, AREDIT, A BRANCH OF PRESSES DE LA CITÉ)

As de cœur (1962–1963)
Bagatelle (1966)
Calypso (?)
Caracas (1964–1966)
Célia (1962–1963)
Ciné Flash (1966)
Cinévision (1962)
Copacabana (1964–1966)
Corail (1964)
Miroir du cœur (1959?–1963?) (initially published by Edital/Artima)
Quiproquo (1966)
Romantic (1962)

ARTURO MERCURIO

Avec Toi (1959–1962)
Ciné sélection (1958–1962)
Ciné succès (1958–1962)
Étoile d'amour (1960; later, Lancio)
Mon cœur (1960–?)
Toi et moi (1958–1962)

BOZZESI

Deux Télé Romans Épopée (1963)
Deux Télé Romans Jungle (1963)
Les Films du cœur (1959–1965)
Les Films pour vous (1956–1963)
Star Ciné Aventures (1958–1973)
Star Ciné Bravoure (1961–1973)
Star Ciné Colt (1969–1973; published later in the run by Cavaglia)
Star Ciné Cosmos (1961–1965)
Star Ciné Roman (1956–1965)
Star Ciné Vaillance (1961–1965)
Star Ciné Winchester (1969–1973; published later in the run by Cavaglia)
Votre Film (1962–1963)

EDISIRIO (LATER PONZONI)

Jungle Films (1960–1968)
Western Aventures (1961–1962?)

ÉDITIONS DES REMPARTS

Amor Film (1957–1963)

LES ÉDITIONS MONDIALES

Mon amour (1957?–1959?)
Nous Deux Film (1956–1962?)
Nous Deux présente: Aventures Actions (1960?–1962?)
Nous Deux présente: Festival Film (1956?–1961?)
Nous Deux présente: Film Moderne (1957?–1959?)
Nous Deux présente: Roman Film Étoile (1957?–1962?)
Nous Deux présente: Roman Film Série d'or (1959?–1960?)
Nous Deux présente: Roman Film Vedette (1959?–1964?)
Vie heureuse (1958?–1963?)

EDITOR (LATER ÉDITIONS MONDIALES)

Ciné-Révélation (1957–1963)

MON FILM (1924–1967)

Mon Film (1957–1967)
Mon Film Spécial (1958–1959)

PONZONI (SEE ALSO VICTORY AND EDISIRIO)

Attaque (1966–1967)
Aventures de cape et d'épée (1962)
Cow Boy Magazine (1964–1968)
Far West magazine (around 1967)
Paras (1967–1968)
Photo Aventures (1958–1968)
Les Récits du shérif (1963–1968)
Wampir (1967)
Zatan roi de la jungle (1964–1965?)

SKANDIA

Film Horreur (?)
UFO (?)
West (?)
Western (1967?–1971?)

LA TORRACCIA

Les Films pour vous (1956–1963?)
Roman Film Color (1958–1962)
Roman Film d'amour et d'aventures (1956–1962)
Roman Film: Un Film pour vous (1957–1958?)

VICTORY (LATER EDISIRIO, THEN PONZONI)

Amours à l'écran (1962)
Hebdo Roman (1956–1961)
Pages d'amour (1963?)
Photo Roman (1955–1964)
Roman d'amour (1961–1963)
Votre roman (1957–1963)
Western Aventures (1961–1963?)

Italy

Main sources: Silvio Alovisio, ed., *La Collezione del Museo Nazionale del Cinema*, Museo Nazionale del Cinema, 2007; and Emiliano Morreale, ed., *Gianni Amelio presenta Lo Schermo di Carta*, Museo Nazionale del Cinema / Il Castoro, 2007.

AVA

I grandi amori dello schermo (1954–1956)
I grandi drammi dello schermo (1954–1956)
I grandi spettacoli dello schermo (1954–1956)
I grandi successi dello schermo (1954–1956)

BOZZESI

Star cineromanzo gigante (1955–1956)

I vostri film (1956–1956)
Super Star cineromanzo gigante (1956–1964)

FEDORA BELLIS (?)

Tutti i romanzi d'amore (1958–1960?)

GIOGGI

I Cineromanzi celebri (1956)
Il Cineromanzo economico (1955–1956)

IMO

I vostri film-romanzo (1954–1964)

LANCIO

Stelle cineromanzi (1959–1964)

LANTERNA MAGICA

Cineromanzi per tutti (1954–1957)
Cineromanzo gigante (1955–1957)
Orsa maggiore (1956–1956)

NOVISSIMA

I Film di cine illustrato (1954–1958?)

LA TORRACCIA

Cinefoto (Cine Foto Romanzo). Un Film per voi (1955–1961)
Roman Film Color (1958–1961)

VICTORY (LATER EDISIRIO, LATER PONZONI)

Grandi fotoromanzi d'amore (1952–1957)
Fotoromanzo bimensile (1954–1957)
Fotoromanzo gigante (Victory) (1954–1957)

Spain

EDICIONES MANDOLINA

Ciné Ensueño (1959)

United Kingdom

C. ARTHUR PEARSON LTD.

Continental Film Photo Stories (1960)
TV Photo Stories (1958–1959)

United States

JAMES WARREN PUBLICATIONS

Famous Films (1964–1965)

Notes

Chapter 1: Excavating the Film Photonovel

1. The term "*fumetti*," Italian for "comics" (the word *fumetti* literally means "little puffs of smoke," a reference to speech balloons) is used as a synonym for photonovel. As happens in other linguistic areas, US English does not distinguish the photonovel from the film photonovel (*fotoromanzo* and *cineromanzo*, respectively, in Italian, but even here the terminology is subject to a large dose of creative anarchy).
2. An interesting case of cultural self-hatred and self-castigation of the photonovel and the related film and film-photonovel businesses is *La Lacrima nel pugno* (1957), a roman à clef by Liala, a famous Italian romance writer who worked a great deal in the photonovel industry (Cardone 2004a, 156).
3. High-art continuations of the genre, such as Bruce Mau's reinterpretation of the cult film by Chris Marker, *La Jetée / The Jetty* (Marker 1993), are briefly discussed at the end of this book.
4. It was republished in French by the same publisher, Bozzesi, in the *Star Ciné Roman* series as *Ulysse* (issue 54, 1 March 1959).
5. The conversion rate of the Italian lire and the French franc to current values can be found here: Currency Converter in the Past, http://fxtop.com/en/currency-converter-past.php?A=30&C1=ITL&C2=USD&DD=01&MM=02&YYYY=1955&B=1&P=&I=1&btnOK=Go%21 (Italy), and http://www.bdm

.insee.fr/bdm2/affichageSeries.action?idbank=001643154&page=tableau&codeGroupe=1391&recherche=idbank (France). Thirty Italian lire in 1955 were the equivalent of 0.46 euros in 2014 (US$0.54 in 2018). One hundred French francs in 1957 were the equivalent of 2 euros in 2017 (US$2.34 in 2018).

6. My thanks to Geert Buelens, who brought this point to my attention. These works were published in the weekly *Die Huisgenoot*, which still exists: http://www.huisgenoot.com.
7. In the early 1980s, Greantori Publishers (Paris) released triweekly installments, each of them fifty to sixty pages long, which were later gathered in groups of three into several albums. In the late 1950s in the United Kingdom, where the film photonovel seems to have been less popular, there were some initiatives to launch a similar format based on recent TV serials. A key player was the magazine *TV Photo Series*, which published serials such as *O.S.S.* (Office of Strategic Services) and *William Tell*, using the double slogan (one on top and one at the bottom of the front cover): "Told in *REAL* PHOTOS just as you see it" and "*Your TV favourites in PHOTOGRAPHS that live*!" The same London publisher, C. Arthur Pearson Ltd., published *T.V. Picture Stories*, which used similar slogans: "An Exciting Story All in Pictures" and "A New T.V. Picture Story Every Week." According to the Grand Comics Database, sixty issues were published in 1958–1959 (https://www.comics.org/series/56735). According to the same source, only two issues were published, both in 1960, in the series *Continental Film Photo Stories* (https://www.comics.org/series/67283/).
8. The historical importance of this "secondary" material has been increasingly recognized by film scholars; for instance, the "film novel" can be a way of accessing scenes that were excised from the final cut (see Bassano 2007 for the example of Fellini's *La Strada*). As we will see, what applies to the film novel and the novelization is also valid for the film photonovel, which is anything but a simple "copy" of the existing movie.

Chapter 2: A Brief History of the Film Photonovel

1. I use the notion of "paratext" as defined by Gérard Genette (1997). But I do not take into account the second half of Genette's definition, which distinguishes between "peritext" (this is generally how the umbrella term "paratext" is understood) and "epitext," that is, the comments made by the author on her or his work outside the book (interviews, diaries, correspondence, and so forth). I limit myself to the "paratext" as "peritext."
2. The political dimension of the "utopian" character of daydreaming and evasion has been disclosed, however, by Richard Dyer in a famous anti-Adorno study (Dyer 1992) on the Hollywood musical. Dyer's work has been key in scholars' growing responsiveness to the audience's "appropriationist" approach to mass culture.

3. The title is an overt allusion to a collection of love poetry, *Toi et Moi* (You and me), by Paul Géraldy (1912), still in print in French and often quoted as the typical example of low-middlebrow confessional love poetry.
4. It was for *Bolero-Film* that the label "*fotoromanzo*," or photonovel, was coined. *Il Mio Sogno* announced the new genre via a paraphrasing self-definition: "*settimanale di romanzi d'amore a fotogrammi*," literally, "weekly magazine of romance novels with photographs." The question of the paternity of the genre remains unanswered, although historians tend to settle on Cesare Zavattini, a key player in the neorealist movement (Bravo 2003). For a cultural history of the photonovel, see the works by Abruzzese (1989) and Fiorentino (2013), who underscore the "range" of the medium, much broader than that of film, which was present only in urban areas.
5. This is well known to all Tintin lovers, who still find a mention of this law in small print at the back of all the albums.
6. As far as I know, the complete list includes the following works: *The General* (Buster Keaton), *Casablanca* (Michael Curtiz), *Dr. Jekyll and Mr. Hyde* (Rouben Mamoulian), *Frankenstein* (James Whale), *Stagecoach* (John Ford), and *Ninotchka* (Billy Wilder). *Psycho* (Alfred Hitchcock) and *The Maltese Falcon* (John Huston) were edited by the same Anobile, but published by Picador.
7. *Les Visiteurs du soir* (Marcel Carné), *La Grande Illusion* (Jean Renoir), *Drôle de drame* (Marcel Carné), *À bout de souffle* (Jean-Luc Godard), and *La Belle et la Bête* (Jean Cocteau).
8. Later counterexamples such as Ado Kyrou's *An Honest Man* and Chris Marker and Bruce Mau's *The Jetty* originated in a completely different cultural context, whose readers may have never heard of the existence of the popular film photonovel. They are briefly touched on in the last section of this book.
9. Very lowbrow publications did not refrain from endlessly reusing pictures of stars who were linked with a certain genre but completely absent from the story itself; see, for example, the many cover illustrations featuring Clint Eastwood in the weekly output of film photonovel magazines such as *Cow Boy Magazine*.
10. For more detailed information, see Ghera (2006), who gives a complete overview of all the film photonovels published by *Mon Film*.
11. The format and the number of pages were not always the same, but the editorial policy of the magazine proved remarkably stable.
12. Those interested in the field seem to accept that in some cases, less well-established or ephemeral magazines did not ask for any authorization whatsoever. The absence of some companies' films from film-photonovel catalogues, however, seems to suggest that, in principle, adaptation rights were cleared—and that certain companies (actually, a minority) were less eager than others to play the game. Some details on this trade can be found in the oral-history testimony of Michele Mercuri (2007), who insists on the

freelance status of the intermediaries who had to obtain the film-photonovel rights for the magazine releases, and on the relatively small direct financial benefits for the film producers and distributors. It is hoped that further archival research will unearth details of the contracts that resulted from these negotiations.

13. Raffaele De Berti (2000, 139) discusses the subscription prices of the Italian magazines, in comparison with those of the film-novel magazines of the mid-1950s: the photonovel magazines *Grand Hôtel* (1,500 lire), *Bolero-Film* (1,750 lire), and *Sogno* (1,350 lire) were less expensive than *Novelle Film* (2,200 lire). His comparison does not include subscription prices for film-photonovel magazines, which is not surprising, given the publishers' emphasis on newsstand sales; for example, in 1955 the flagship series *Star Ciné Roman* did not even mention the possibility of getting a subscription.
14. Certain middlebrow photonovel magazines of the 1970s, such as the Belgian *Femmes d'Aujourd'hui* (Modern women), included reports on the shooting of upcoming works, interviews with directors and actors, analyses of the social and cultural relevance of the production, and so forth, exactly as if the difference between a film set and a photonovel set no longer existed.
15. A strange example, that of *Amor Film*, is discussed in chapter 4.
16. On the contact and transition zone between the film novel and the film photonovel in Italy, see De Berti (2000).
17. The first two movies starred Gina Lollobrigida (always next to De Sica). Excerpts of the film-photonovel version of these three historically important films are analyzed in chapter 4.
18. The layout principles and marketing structure of this film photonovel are so unusual that it is implausible to consider this Spanish edition a mere translation of the Italian version published in *Cine Selezione Mondiale* (vol. 2, no. 16, 1955). Some features of the Spanish work are discussed in chapter 6.
19. A typical example is Antonella Lualdi, whose success in the movie industry, thanks to *Abbiamo vinto!* (1951), explains why the photonovel in which she stars, "Mio figlio è soltanto mio" (1949), was published only in 1951, in a version that partially hides her identity (she is credited under the pseudonym Arabella Ingres).
20. My sincerest thanks to Alain Boillat, whose work on the Autant-Lara archives has disclosed a fascinating detail of the contract signed between the producer (Iéna) and the director (Autant-Lara) for *En Cas de malheur* (1958) (personal communication). The contract is both precise and vague: it excludes the director from all derived rights, except for "un récit illustré en langue française, d'après le film genre dit 'film-complet,' mais qui ne devra pas excéder 7.000 mots" (an illustrated story in French, similar to the genre named "complete film," but which cannot be longer than 7,000 words). Although the contract seems to apply only to a certain type of short, lowbrow film novelization, it is possible to imagine that it also applies to film-photonovel adaptations. There was such an adaptation in *Mon Film* (May 1959).

After that, this magazine merged with *Le Film complet*, its productions shifted from the film novel to the film-photonovel format. For a more general presentation of this research, see Boillat and Philippe (2018).

21. The author's private collection lists nine items for 20th Century–Fox (including *Island in the Sun*, Robert Rossen, 1957, and *The Long Hot Summer*, Martin Ritt, 1958) and eleven items for Universal (including *Tarantula*, Jack Arnold, 1955, and *Lover Come Back*, Delbert Mann, 1961). These items are in French and may not exist in Italian. But given the relatively large number of these adaptations, it is not plausible to believe that all of them were unauthorized or semiclandestine works, although those also existed, as, for instance, in the extremely cheap and most lowbrow segment of the market.
22. Just one example: the number of films starring Kim Novak or Anthony Perkins, not to speak of European stars such as Sophia Loren or Gina Lollobrigida, was absolutely breathtaking in these years.
23. The situation of the French market differed not only because the ultimate "Italianness" of Matarazzo's work made it less easily exportable to other countries but also because the Matarazzo hype had already strongly declined when the film photonovel entered France, hence the belated film-photonovel adaptations of the famous Matarazzo trilogy: *Catene* ("Je suis innocent!") was published in 1961, *Tormento* ("Tourments") in 1962, and *I Figli di nessuno* ("Fils de personne") in 1961. All three works appeared in rather lowbrow series.
24. Some examples are *Mon Cœur* (Mercurio) and *Toi et Moi* (Lancio).
25. Exceptionally, a film photonovel may also work with film stills that did not make it till the final cut. For an example of the already mentioned Matarazzo vehicle *Catene*, see Cardone (2004b) for an analysis of this "supplementary footage," and Quaresima (2004) for a more general reflection on the (never documented) possibility of an "autonomous" shooting of the film photonovel as a kind of second version of the director's final cut.

Chapter 3: Word and Image, Telling and Showing

1. An in-depth reading of this work is given in chapter 5.
2. As is well known, this is the key theme of Fellini's *The White Sheik* (1952), which presents a satire—a rather mild one—on the entangled worlds of cinema and photonovels.
3. Duration of the fragment: 0:26–1:04. Available on YouTube: https://www.youtube.com/watch?v=LjOuCMfBJZY.
4. "La Garçonnière," *Les Films du Cœur*, Bozzesi, 1961.
5. My analysis in chapter 5 of the adaptation of the 1958 Louis Malle movie *Ascenseur pour l'échafaud* (*Elevator to the Gallows*) insists on the power of a certain minimalist approach.
6. In some cases, these text panels contain smaller or larger illustrations,

some of them purely decorative, others clearly referring to the theme of the work. Their function is aesthetic as well as narrative: they are panel fillers, but also point toward the key motifs of the work.

7. It is the same publisher that confuses *i* and *y*.
8. The dating is based on Ghera (2006) and was checked against the available corpus.
9. On the political dimension of this strategy, see the polemic launched by François Truffaut ([1954] 1967) at the dawn of the New Wave era.
10. Unlike what happens in very lowbrow series such as *Avec Toi* or *Étoile d'amour*, both published by Mercurio, in which the reissue of older films in film-photonovel format discloses the difficulties of the publisher in obtaining the rights to successful contemporary films, the choice by *Nous Deux Film* of a classic was a purposeful attempt to upgrade the prestige of the series.
11. I am using the translation in the restored version produced by the Centre National de l'Audiovisuel, Luxembourg, and Célia Films (original producer: Janus Films; current edition: Criterion Collection).
12. A previous novel, *Un Barrage contre le Pacifique* (1950; translated in 1952 as *The Sea Wall*), was adapted in 1957 (released in 1958) by René Clément, a well-respected but more traditionally inspired director of upscale mainstream French cinema. Starring Silvana Mangano and Anthony Perkins, and produced by Columbia and Dino De Laurentiis, this film was not written by Duras.
13. One might think of the clear-line aesthetics here, which exceeds the domain of comics and cartooning.

Chapter 4: Clear Grids, Blurred Lines

1. This is a page of the Italian original, as reproduced in the study by Fiorentino (1996). The two French versions of this work (in *Star Ciné Roman* and *Ciné Sélection*) present some variations, mainly because of the different use of larger-format photos, and unfortunately, they lose the special tabularity effect of the Italian version.
2. In the Hemingway chapter of *Why Read the Classics?,* Italo Calvino ([1991] 2000, 224) gives the following description of Hemingway's appeal: "Actually, to be truthful, it was the twin constellation of Hemingway and Malraux that attracted me, the symbol of international antifascism, the international front in the Spanish Civil War. Fortunately we Italians had had D'Annunzio to inoculate us against certain 'heroic' inclinations, and the rather aestheticizing base to Malraux's work soon became apparent. (For some people in France, such as Roger Vailland, who is also a very nice guy, a bit superficial but genuine enough, the Hemingway-Malraux double-bill was a formative factor.)"
3. According to Isabella Antonutti (2013), this pursuit of status was a lifelong concern of the working-class Italian immigrant Cino Del Duca, who

endowed a lavish literary prize, which no serious writer dared to accept, and whose participation in the film production business was amazing, to say the least. He coproduced, for instance, Antonioni's *L'Avventura* (1960), a milestone of existentialist New Wave cinema, while also taking care of the first "restoration" (according to contemporary standards, it would be called a mutilation) of *The Passion of Joan of Arc* by Carl Dreyer (1928).

4. Among other means, there were all kinds of "reader's digest" novelizations of the movies. See, for instance, the (anonymous) writing in basic French of *La Chartreuse de Parme: Un film de Christian-Jacque adapté du roman de Stendhal* (Paris: Self, 1948). The film's screenplay was by Pierre Véry. These simplified and abridged novelizations of movies that were themselves based on sometimes very complex literary works were not unusual in this period (Baetens 2008).
5. On the political agenda of film adaptations, see the pamphlet by François Truffaut ([1954] 1967) and the critical rereading in Boillat and Philippe (2018).
6. Present-day readers may consider this pose rather counterproductive, but the Napoleonic myth was still very strong in the postwar years. What strikes us today as unintentionally ironic, even ridiculous, was certainly intended to be taken seriously. Many other aspects of the film-photonovel culture of these years must have undergone similar shifts in the audience's perception (the implicit sexism of much material is a case in point).
7. The list of adapted movies includes *Battle Hymn* (Douglas Sirk, 1957), *Island in the Sun* (Robert Rossen, 1957), *The Sheriff of Fractured Jaw* (Raoul Walsh, 1958), and *Rally 'round the Flag, Boys!* (Leo McCarey, 1958). This list bluntly contradicts the idea that *Amor Film* specialized in B movies.

Chapter 5: Action? Stop! Pose and Movement

1. He appeared also in the fourth and last work of the series, the very disappointing *Bread, Love and Andalusia* (1958), which is set in Spain and not considered part of the *Bread and Love* trilogy.

Chapter 6: Globalizing the Film Photonovel?

1. For linguistic reasons, I am unfortunately obliged to bracket the Asian production. The few examples of Chinese film photonovels I have had the chance to purchase—and even to read, thanks to translations provided by Kin Wai (Amelia) Chu—suggest that this production is definitely worth analyzing.
2. For Chile, see the portal site *Fotonovela Chilena*, www.fotonovelachilena.cl.
3. In *Secretos* (editorial Creaciones, Buenos Aires), no. 422, 4 August 1958, one finds four photonovel installments as well as the film photonovel "Nacida

en marzo," an adaptation of the movie *Nata di marzo* (Antonio Pietrangeli, 1958).

4. The six pages can be seen at Bhob Stewart, "Topps #8: Bonnie and Clyde Fumetti," *Potrzebie*, 9 April 2010, http://potrzebie.blogspot.be/2010/04/bonnie-and-clyde-fumetti.html.
5. Ibid.
6. First published in *La Révolution surréaliste* 12, 15 December 1929, 72–73. The work, by René Magritte, presents a set of photo-booth pictures of the Parisian surrealists spread around a painting of a naked woman, in the style of a board game.
7. See, for instance, the central place of both the film and the film photonovel in the thematic exhibition on the photonovel organized by the Musée des civilisations de l'Europe et de la Méditerranée in Marseille (December 2017; curators Marie-Charlotte Calafat and Frédérique Deschamps).
8. The American remake of the movie, Terry Gilliam's *Twelve Monkeys* (1995), bears no relation to the original work. The category of pseudo-remake, were it to exist, would perfectly apply to this reinterpretation of Marker's film.

References

Primary Sources

"L'Adorable Voisine" (*Bell, Book and Candle*, 1958, Richard Quine). *Les Films pour vous*, 7 January 1961.

"L'Amant fantôme" (*Pandora and the Flying Dutchman*, 1951, Albert Lewin). *Photo Roman*, February 1959.

"Arizona" (original unknown). *Cow Boy Magazine*, February 1966.

"Ascenseur pour l'échafaud" (*Ascenseur pour l'échafaud*, 1958, Louis Malle). *Mon Film*, October 1960.

"La Belle et la bête" (*La Belle et la bête*, 1946, Jean Cocteau). *Nous Deux présente Roman Film Vedette*, April–June 1959.

"La Chartreuse de Parme" (*La Chartreuse de Parme*, 1948, Christian-Jacque). *Nous Deux Film*, April–June 1961.

"Cœurs en détresse" (*El Indiano*, 1955, Fernando Soler). *Miroir du cœur*, September 1959.

"Cuori vagabondi" (Grazia Maria Francia). *Il Mio Sogno*, 2 May 1948.

"The Curse of Frankenstein." *Famous Films #2* [actually #3], 1965.

"L'Enquête mystérieuse" (*The Frightened City*, 1961, John Lemont). *Amor Film*, 1 July 1962.

"La Finestra sul cortile" (*Rear Window*, 1954, Alfred Hitchcock). *Star Cineromanzo Gigante*, 30 June 1955.

"La Fureur de vivre" (*Rebel Without a Cause*, 1955, Nicholas Ray). *Star Ciné Roman*, 1 November 1958.

"Hélène de Troie" (*Helen of Troy*, 1956, Robert Wise). *Star Ciné Roman*, 1 July 1958.

"La Loi" (*La Legge*, 1959, Jules Dassin). *Nous Deux Film*, July–September 1959.

Marker, Chris. 1993. *The Jetty*. New York: Zone.

"Moderato cantabile" (*Moderato Cantabile*, 1960, Peter Brook). *Mon Film*, December 1960.

"Monte-Carlo" (*The Monte Carlo Story*, 1957, Sam Taylor / Giulio Macchi). *Ciné Succès*, July 1962.

"Las Noches de Cabiria" (*Le Notti de Cabiria*, 1957, Federico Fellini). *Cine Ensueño*, 1959, six installments.

"Pain, amour, ainsi soit-il" (*Pane, amore e . . .*, 1955, Dino Risi). *Star Ciné Roman*, 15 March 1961.

"Pain, amour et . . ." (*Pane, amore e . . .*, 1955, Dino Risi). *Ciné Sélection*, September 1962.

"Pane, amore e . . ." (*Pane, amore e . . .*, 1955, Dino Risi). Original source unknown.

"La Piste des éléphants" (*Elephant Walk*, 1954, William Dieterle). *Star Ciné Roman*, 15 February 1958.

"La Princesse de Clèves" (*La Princesse de Clèves*, 1961, Jean Delannoy). *Nous Deux Film*, April–June 1961.

"Revoir Florence" (*Porta un bacione a Firenze*, 1955, Camillo Mastrocinque). *Roman Film*, 15 April 1958.

"Stagecoach" (John Ford, 1939). In *John Ford's Stagecoach*, edited by Richard J. Anobile. New York: Darien House, 1975.

Stewart, Bhob. 1968. "Bonnie and Clyde." In *The Bonnie and Clyde Scrapbook*, n.p. New York: Personality Posters, 1968.

"Les Voies du Coeur" (*Le vie del cuore*, 1942, Camillo Mastrocinque). *Ciné Succès*, August 1961.

"La Voix de la conscience" (*Crimen y castigo*, 1951, Fernando de Fuentes). *Hebdo Roman*, 20 July 1960.

"Volupté" (*Go Naked in the World*, 1961, Ranald MacDougall). *Les Films du coeur*, 5 December 1963.

Secondary Sources

Abruzzese, Alberto. 1989. "Fotoromanzo." In *Letteratura italiana: Storia e geografia*, vol. 3, *L'età contemporanea*, edited by Alberto Asor Rosa, 1269–1287. Turin: Einaudi.

Alovisio, Silvio, ed. 2007. *Cineromanzi: La collezione del Museo Nazionale del Cinema*. Turin: Museo Nazionale del Cinema.

Amelio, Gianni. 2007. "Non voglio perderti." In *Gianni Amelio presenta Lo Schermo di carta: Storia e storia dei cineromanzi*, edited by Emiliano Morreale, 11–17. Turin: Museo Nazionale del Cinema / Il Castoro.

Antonutti, Isabelle. 2013. *Cino Del Duca: De* Tarzan *à* Nous Deux*; Itinéraire d'un patron de presse.* Rennes: Presses Universitaires de Rennes.

Baetens, Jan. 2005. "Novelization: A Contaminated Genre?" *Critical Inquiry* 32, no. 1: 43–60.

———. 2008. *La Novellisation: Du Film au roman.* Brussels: Les Impressions Nouvelles. Published in English as *Novelization: From Film to Novel.* Translated by Mary Feeney. Columbus: Ohio State University Press.

———. 2010. *Pour le roman-photo.* Brussels: Les Impressions Nouvelles.

———. 2013. "The Photonovel: Stereotype as Surprise." *History of Photography* 37, no. 2: 137–152.

———. 2015. "Adapting and Displaying Multiple Temporalities: What Became of Trollope's *John Caldigate* and Maupassant's *Boule de Suif* in Simon Grennan (*Dispossession*) and Battaglia (*Contes et nouvelles de guerre*)." In *Transforming Anthony Trollope: Dispossession, Victorianism and Nineteenth-Century Word and Image*, edited by Lawrence Grove and Simon Grennan, 15–32. Leuven, Belgium: Leuven University Press.

———. 2016. "'Sur place': La poétique du transport dans *La Belle et la Bête: Journal d'un film.*" In *Jean Cocteau*, edited by Serge Linares, 457–465. Paris: Cahiers de l'Herne.

———. 2017a. "Le ciné-photo-roman ou cineromanzo: Une novellisation singulière." In *Le Cinéma de la littérature*, edited by Jean Cléder and Frank Wagner, 77–92. Nantes: Éditions Nouvelles Cécile Defaut.

———. 2017b. "The Drawn Novel." In "Bande Dessinée out of the Box," edited by Laurence Grove. Special issue, *Yale French Studies* 131–132:65–83.

Baetens, Jan, Johan Callens, Michel Delville, Bertrand Gervais, Heidi Peeters, Robyn Warhol, and Myriam Watthee-Delmotte. 2015. "LMI/Genre/Medium: A Research Update." *Germanisch Romanische Monatsschrift* 64, no. 4: 485–492.

Baetens, Jan, and Stefania Giovenco. 2014. "Le roman-photo: Images d'une histoire." *Arabeschi* 4:178–202.

Bassano, Roberta. 2007. "Cineromanzi per giganti: Senso e La Strada." In *Gianni Amelio presenta Lo Schermo di Carta: Storia et storie dei cineromanzi*, edited by Emiliano Morreale, 87–95. Turin: Museo Nazionale di Cinema / Il Castoro.

Beaty, Bart, and Benjamin Woo. 2016. *The Greatest Comic Book of All Time: Symbolic Capital and the Field of American Comic Books.* London: Palgrave Macmillan.

Boillat, Alain, and Gilles Philpe, eds. 2018. *L'Adaptation: Des livres aux scénarios.* Brussels: Les Impressions Nouvelles.

Bolter, Jay David, and Richard Grusin. 1999. *Remediation: Understanding New Media.* Cambridge, MA: MIT Press.

Bonifazio, Paola. 2017. "Political Photoromances: The Italian Communist Party, *Famiglia Cristiana*, and the Struggle for Women's Hearts." *Italian Studies* 72, no. 4: 393–413.

Bravo, Ana. 2003. *Il Fotoromanzo.* Bologna: Il Mulino.

Brooks, Peter. (1976) 1995. *The Melodramatic Imagination*. New Haven, CT: Yale University Press.

Burgin, Victor. 2004. *The Remembered Film*. London: Reaktion Books.

Calafat, Marie-Charlotte, and Frédérique Deschamps, eds. 2017. *Roman-photo*. Paris: Textuel and Mucem.

Calvino, Italo. (1991) 2000. *Why Read the Classics?* Translated by Martin McLaughlin. London: Vintage.

Capart, Philippe. 2015. "Les Patrons de la bande dessinée." *La Crypte Tonique* 12:5–21.

Cardone, Lucia. 2004a. *Con lo schermo nel cuore: Grand Hôtel e il cinema (1946–1956)*. Pisa: Edizione ETS.

———. 2004b. "*Catene amare*: Un cineromanzo tra film e teatro." *Bianco e nero* 548:71–77.

———. 2006. "'Il discorso amoroso'" dello schermo alla carta: La rappresentazione delle passioni nei cineromanzi degli anni Cinquanta." In *Il racconto del film / Narrating the Film*, edited by Alice Autelitano and Valentina Re, 241–258. Udine, Italy: Forum.

Carrillo, Loretta, and Thomas A. Lyson. 1983. "The *Fotonovela* as a Cultural Bridge for Hispanic Women in the United States." *Journal of Popular Cultures* 17, no. 3: 59–64.

Cavell, Stanley. 1979. *The World Viewed: Reflections on the Ontology of Film*. Cambridge, MA: Harvard University Press.

Chabrier, Amélie. 2013. "Les Mystères de New-York: Stratégies d'adaptation d'un serial américain au pays de l'oncle Sue." In "Les Mystères urbains au prisme de l'identité nationale," edited by Marie-Ève Thérenty, n.p. Special issue, *Médias* 19. www.medias19.org/index.php?id=13613.

Cinegrafie, no. 20, 2007. *Matarazzo: Romanzi popolari / Popular Romances*. Bologna: Cineteca Bologna / Le Mani.

Cohen, Nadja. 2016. *Fondane et le cinéma*. Paris: Jean-Michel Place.

Collins, Jim. 2010. *Bring On the Books for Everybody: How Literary Culture Became Popular Culture*. Durham, NC: Duke University Press.

Cooke, Jon B., and David Roach. 2001. *The Warren Companion*. Raleigh, NC: TwoMorrows.

Curiel, Fernando. 1990. *Fotonovela rosa, fotonovela roja*. Mexico City: Universidad Nacional Autónoma de Mexico.

de Baecque, Antoine. (2002) 2013. *La Cinéphilie: Invention d'un regard, histoire d'une culture, 1944–1968*. Paris: Fayard/Pluriel.

De Berti, Raffaele. 2000. *Dallo schermo alla carta: Romanzi, fotoromanzi, rotocalchi cinematografici; Il film e i suoi paratesti*. Milan: Vita e Pensiero.

———. 2004. "Leggere il film." *Bianco e nero* 548:19–25.

De Falco, Cristina. 2004. "*Las Noches de Cabiria*: Da racconto poetico a racconto moraleggiante." *Bianco e nero* 548:79–85.

De Kosnik, Abigail. 2016. *Rogue Archives: Digital Cultural Memory and Media Fandom*. Cambridge, MA: MIT Press.

Dyer, Richard. 1992. *Only Entertainment*. London: Routledge.

Edwards, Nikki. 2016. "Fotonovela." In *The Rural Women's Health Project*. www.rwhp.org/fotonovela.html.

Egoyan, Atom, and Balfour, Ian, eds. 2004. *Subtitles: On the Foreignness of Film*. Cambridge, MA: Alphabet City / MIT Press.

Elsaesser, Thomas. 2009. "The Return of 3D." *Critical Inquiry* 39, no. 2: 217–246.

Faber, Dominique, Marion Minuit, and Bruno Takodjerad. 2012. *Nous Deux présente: La Saga du roman-photo*. Paris: Jean-Claude Gawsewitch.

Faulkner, Christopher. 2008. "The Phenomenon of the *Film Raconté* and the Novelizations of *La Règle du jeu*." *South Central Review* 25, no. 2: 22–44.

Fiorentino, Giovanni, ed. 1995. *Luci del Sud: Sorrento un set per Sofia*. Napoli: Eidos.

———. 2013. "Il mosaico delle immagini: Gli anni Cinquanta ai bordi del consumo." In *Consumi e mass media*, edited by Francesca Anania, 11–51. Bologna: Il Mulino.

Fresnault-Deruelle, Pierre. 1976. "Du linéaire au tabulaire." *Communications* 24:7–23.

Frey, Hugo. 2014. *Nationalism and the Cinema in France: Political Mythologies and Film Events, 1945–1995*. Oxford: Berghahn.

Gaudreault, André. 2009. *From Plato to Lumière: Narration and Monstration in Literature and Cinema*. Toronto: Toronto University Press.

Gaudreault, André, and Philippe Marion. (2013) 2015. *The End of Cinema? A Medium in Crisis in the Digital Age*. Translated by Timothy Barnard. New York: Columbia University Press.

Genette, Gérard. (1987) 1997. *Paratexts: Thresholds of Interpretation*. Translated by Jane E. Lewin. Cambridge: Cambridge University Press.

———. 2004. *Métalepse: De la figure à la fiction*. Paris: Seuil.

Ghera, Serge. 2006. *Ciné-romans*. http://bmania.pagesperso-orange.fr/index.html.

Giet, Sylvette. 1997. *Nous Deux, 1947–1997: Apprendre la langue du coeur*. Leuven, Belgium / Paris: Peeters/Vrin.

Groensteen, Thierry. (1999) 2009. *The System of Comics*. Translated by Bart Beaty and Nick Nguyen. Jackson: University Press of Mississippi.

Hatfield, Charles. 2005. *Alternative Comics*. Jackson: University Press of Mississippi.

Hayles, N. Katherine, and Jessica Pressman, eds. 2013. *Comparative Textual Media: Transforming the Humanities in the Postprint Era*. Minneapolis: University of Minnesota Press.

Herner, Irene. 1979. *Mitos y onitors: Historietas y Fotonovelas en Mexico*. Mexico City: Universidad Nacional Autónoma de Mexico.

Hesmondhalgh, David. 2013. *The Cultural Industries*. London: Sage.

Hoelzl, Ingrid, and Remi Marie. 2015. *Softimage: Towards a New Theory of the Digital Image*. Bristol, UK: Intellect.

Jacobs, Steven. 2010. "The History and Aesthetics of the Classical Film Still." *History of Photography* 34, no. 4: 373–386.

Jeannelle, Jean-Louis. (2013) 2016. "Adaptability: Literature and Cinema Redux." *Studies in French Cinema* 16, no. 2: 95–105.
Jenkins, Henry. 2006. *Convergence Culture: Where Old and New Media Collide.* New York: New York University Press.
Labarre, Nicolas. 2017. *"Heavy Metal": L'autre "Métal Hurlant."* Bordeaux: Presses Universitaires de Bordeaux.
Leonardi, Francesca. 2006. "La Vie passionnée des *Cousins*: Les avatars d'un film Nouvelle Vague." In *Il racconto del film / Narrating the Film*, edited by Alice Autelitano and Valentina Re, 179–195. Udine, Italy: Forum.
Lessing, G. E. (1766) 1984. *Laocoon: An Essay on the Limits of Painting and Poetry.* Translated by Edward Allen McCormick. Baltimore: Johns Hopkins University Press.
Letourneux, Matthieu. 2015. *Cinéma: Premiers crimes.* Paris: Paris Bibliothèque.
Letourneux, Matthieu, and Jean-Yves Mollier. 2011. *La Librairie Tallandier: Histoire d'une grande maison d'édition populaire, 1870–2000.* Paris: Nouveau Monde.
McCabe, Susan. 2005. *Cinematic Modernism: Modernist Poetry and Film.* New York: Cambridge University Press.
Mercuri, Michele. 2007. "Confidenze di un addetto ai lavori." In *Gianni Amelio presenta Lo Schermo di Carta: Storia et storie dei cineromanzi*, edited by Emiliano Morreale, 212–219. Turin: Museo Nazionale di Cinema / Il Castoro.
Mittell, Jason. 2015. *Complex TV: The Poetics of Contemporary Television Storytelling.* New York: New York University Press.
Morreale, Emiliano, ed. 2007a. *Gianni Amelio presenta Lo Schermo di Carta: Storia et storie dei cineromanzi.* Turin: Museo Nazionale di Cinema / Il Castoro.
———. 2007b. "Il sipario strappato: Introduzione ai cineromanzi." In *Gianni Amelio presenta Lo Schermo di Carta: Storia et storie dei cineromanzi*, edited by Emiliano Morreale, 25–57. Turin: Museo Nazionale di Cinema / Il Castoro.
———. 2007c. "Chi è senza peccato: Cineromanzi alla sbarra." In *Gianni Amelio presenta Lo Schermo di Carta: Storia et storie dei cineromanzi*, edited by Emiliano Morreale, 207–211. Turin: Museo Nazionale di Cinema / Il Castoro.
———. 2007d. "Cronaca di un amore. Conversazione con Gianni Amelio." In *Gianni Amelio presenta Lo Schermo di Carta: Storia et storie dei cineromanzi*, edited by Emiliano Morreale, 227–237. Turin: Museo Nazionale di Cinema / Il Castoro.
———. 2011. *Cosí piangevano: Il cinema melò nell'Italia degli anni cinquanta.* Roma: Donzelli.
Muir, John Kenneth. 2005. "Retro Toy Flashback #16: Photonovels." *John Kenneth Muir's Reflections on Cult Movies and Classic TV.* http://reflectionsonfilmandtelevision.blogspot.be/2005/11/retro-toy-flashback-16-photonovels.html.

Murray, Simone. 2012. *The Adaptation Industry*. London: Routledge.

Paul, William. 2016. *When Movies Were Theatre*. New York: Columbia University Press.

Peterson, Richard A. 1982. "Five Constraints on the Production of Culture: Law, Technology, Market, Organizational Structure, and Occupational Careers." *Journal of Popular Culture* 16, no. 2: 143–153.

Peeters, Benoît. (1988) 2007. "Four Conceptions of the Page." Translated by Jesse Cohn. *ImageText* 3:3. www.english.ufl.edu/imagetext/archives/v3_3/peeters.

———. 1991. *Case, planche, récit*. Paris: Casterman.

Pinchon, Pierre, and Marie-Charlotte Calafat. 2018. *Contrebandes Godard, 1960–1968*. Montreuil, France: Matière.

Quaresima, Leonardo. 2004. "La Voce dello spettatore." *Bianco e nero* 548:29–33.

Ricardou, Jean. 1988. "Éléments de textique (I) (pour une theorie des textures)." *Conséquences* 10:5–37.

Robbe-Grillet, Alain. (1961) 1962. *Last Year at Marienbad*. Translated by Richard Howard. New York: Grove.

———. (1963) 1989. *For a New Novel*. Translated by Richard Howard. Evanston, IL: Northwestern University Press.

Roger, Philippe. (2002) 2005. *The American Enemy*. Translated by Sharon Bowman. Chicago: University of Chicago Press.

Rousseau, Jean-Jacques. (1758) 1967. *Lettre à d'Alembert sur son article "Genève."* Edited by Michel Launay. Paris: GF-Flammarion.

———. (1758) 1968. *Politics and the Arts: Letter to M. D'Alembert on the Theatre.* Translated by Allan Bloom. Ithaca, NY: Cornell University Press.

Sergio, Giuseppe. 2012. *Liala, dal romanzo al fotoromanzo: Le scelte linguistiche, lo stile, i temi*. Milan: Mimesis.

Souchier, Emmanuël. 2007. "Formes et pouvoirs de l'énonciation éditoriale." *Communication et langages* 154:23–38.

Thérenty, Marie-Eve. 2007. *La Littérature au quotidien: Poétiques journalistiques au XIXe siècle*. Paris: Seuil.

Truffaut, François. (1954) 1967. "A Certain Tendency of the French Cinema." *Cahiers du cinéma in English* 1. www.newwavefilm.com/about/a-certain-tendency-of-french-cinema-truffaut.shtml.

Truffaut, François. (1966) 1985. *Hitchcock*. With Helen G. Scott. Rev. ed. New York: Simon and Schuster.

Verstraeten, Peter. 2009. *Film Narratology*. Toronto: Toronto University Press.

Virmaux, Alain, and Odette Virmaux. 1983. *Le ciné-roman*. Paris: Edilig.

Warren Publishing Archive. 2011. https://archive.org/details/warrenpublishing&tab=about.

Williams, Raymond. (1970) 1974. *Television: Technology and Cultural Form*. London: Fontana.

Index